International Marketing and Management Research

Series Editor: **Dr. Anshu Saxena Arora**, Savannah State University, Savannah, GA, USA

Associate Editor: **Amit Arora**, Savannah State University, Savannah, GA, USA

Associate Editor: **Jun Wu**, Savannah State University, Savannah, GA, USA

Copy Editor: **Rebecca Setliff**, Savannah State University, Savannah, GA, USA

Editorial Assistant: **William Proulx**, MBA Student, Savannah State University, Savannah, GA, USA

International Marketing and Management Research presents innovative ideas and new research on understanding the challenges confronting global business. Covering the breadth of international business, articles discuss human management, marketing, leadership, creativity, entrepreneurship. The economic, political, legal, sociocultural, and technological issues related to international business are also discussed. The series provides a forum for academics and professionals to share the latest developments and advances in knowledge and practice of global business and international management. It aims to foster the exchange of ideas on a range of important international subjects and to provide stimulus for research and the further development of international perspectives. The principal aim is to push back the boundaries of the thinking, theory, and practice in international business, global marketing, and management, and to provide a forum to explore these developments. The series publishes research based on theoretical explanations, methodological developments, and modeling.

Books Appearing in This Series:

Anshu Saxena Arora
INTERNATIONAL BUSINESS REALISMS
Globalizing Locally Responsive and Internationally Connected Business Disciplines
Global Logistics & International Business Education and Research Center (G-LIBER)

Anshu Saxena Arora & John R. McIntyre
GLOBAL BUSINESS TRANSCENDENCE
International Perspectives Across Developed and Emerging Economies
Global Logistics & International Business Education and Research Center (G-LIBER)

Anshu Saxena Arora & Sabine Bacouël-Jentjens
ADVERTISING CONFLUENCE
Transitioning Marketing Communications into Social Movements
Global Logistics & International Business Education and Research Center (G-LIBER)

Editorial Review Board:

John McIntyre, CIBER Director, Georgia Institute of Technology, Atlanta, GA, USA

Mostafa Sarhan, Dean, College of Business Administration, Savannah State University, GA, USA

Christophe Crabot, Head of International Affairs, Nottingham Business School, Nottingham Trent University, Nottingham, UK

Sabine Bacouël-Jentjens, Head of International Business & Management Program, ISC Paris Business School, Paris, France

Mahesh S. Raisinghani, Associate Professor of CIS, TWU School of Management, Texas, USA

Nicole Hartley, Lecturer of Marketing, University of Queensland Business School, University of Queensland, Brisbane, Australia

DOI: 10.1057/9781137492265.0001

Petra Molthan-Hill, Team Leader NTU Green Academy Project 'Food for thought', NBS Sustainability Coordinator, Principal Lecturer in Business Sustainability Nottingham Business School, Nottingham Trent University, Nottingham, UK

Reginald Leseane, Associate Dean, Savannah State University, Savannah, GA, USA

D. P. Kothari, Former Director General, J B Group of Institutions, Hyderabad and Former Director, Indian Institute of Technology, India

Gerard Burke, Chair – Department of Logistics and SCM, Georgia Southern University, GA, USA

Hailee Tindale, International Administrative and Pedagogical Manager, ISC Paris Business School, Paris, France

Lisa Yount, Savannah State University, Savannah, GA, USA

Ashwin Malshe, ESSEC Business School, Paris-Singapore

Ulysses Brown, Savannah State University, Savannah, GA, USA

Jun Wu, Savannah State University, Savannah, GA, USA

K. Sivakumar, Lehigh University, Pennsylvania, USA

Satinder Bhatia, Chairperson, Indian Institute of Foreign Trade, New Delhi, India

Bryan Christiansen, Chairman, PRYMARKE, LLC, Michigan, USA and Istanbul, Turkey

Dean Clarke, Business Navigator, IKEA, USA

Ani Agnihotri, USA India Business Summit, Atlanta, USA

Ben Butler, Business Development Executive, SBS Worldwide, Inc, Atlanta

S K Jain, Shri Mata Vaishno Devi University, J & K, India

Sharon Hudson, Advertising Educational Foundation, New York City, NY, USA

Suman Niranjan, Savannah State University, Savannah, GA

Amit Arora, Savannah State University, GA, USA

Niranjan S Kulkarni, Operations Specialist, CRB, Cambridge, MA, USA

A. Banu Goktan Bilhan, University of North Texas at Dallas, Dallas, TX, USA

Puneet Prakash Mathur, Strategy & Operations Consultant, Deloitte Consulting, India

Vishal Gupta, School of Management, State University of New York, Binghamton, NY, USA

Nimit Jain, Sr. Analytics & Visualization Expert, Singapore Consumer Goods, Procter & Gamble, Singapore

GLOBAL LOGISTICS & INTERNATIONAL BUSINESS EDUCATION AND RESEARCH (G-LIBER)

DOI: 10.1057/9781137492265.0001

palgrave▸pivot

Advertising Confluence: Transitioning Marketing Communications into Social Movements

Edited by

▶

Anshu Saxena Arora
Associate Professor of Marketing and Director of Global Logistics and International Business Education Research Center of Excellence, Savannah State University, USA

and

Sabine Bacouël-Jentjens
Professor in Management, ISC Paris Business School, France

DOI: 10.1057/9781137492265.0001

ADVERTISING CONFLUENCE

Copyright © Anshu Saxena Arora and Sabine Bacouël-Jentjens, 2015.
Individual chapters © their respective authors, 2015.
Foreword © John R. McIntyre, 2015

First published in 2015 by
PALGRAVE MACMILLAN®
in the United States—a division of St. Martin's Press LLC,
175 Fifth Avenue, New York, NY 10010.

Where this book is distributed in the UK, Europe and the rest of the world,
this is by Palgrave Macmillan, a division of Macmillan Publishers Limited,
registered in England, company number 785998, of Houndmills,
Basingstoke, Hampshire RG21 6XS.

Palgrave Macmillan is the global academic imprint of the above companies
and has companies and representatives throughout the world.

Palgrave® and Macmillan® are registered trademarks in the United States,
the United Kingdom, Europe and other countries.

ISBN: 978–1–137–49225–8 EPub
ISBN: 978–1–137–49226–5 PDF
ISBN: 978–1–137–49224–1 Hardback

Library of Congress Cataloging-in-Publication Data is available from
the Library of Congress.

A catalogue record of the book is available from the British Library.

First edition: 2015

www.palgrave.com/pivot

DOI: 10.1057/9781137492265

To our Global Marketing and Advertising students for bringing international advertising/marketing ideas, concepts, strategies, campaigns, and above all, Creativity to life...

Dr. Anshu Saxena Arora
Dr. Sabine Bacouël-Jentjens

DOI: 10.1057/9781137492265.0001

Contents

DOI: 10.1057/9781137492265.0001

DOI: 10.1057/9781137492265.0001

List of Figures

DOI: 10.1057/9781137492265.0002

List of Tables

Foreword

John R. McIntyre[1]

> *Global Social Movement Marketing as a Key to Effective Advertising and Branding Strategy: Unleashing the Globalization Potential*

This special issue of the International Marketing and Management Research Series entitled *Advertising Confluence: Transitioning the World of Marketing Communications into Social Movements* is a uniquely positioned contribution of interrelated research papers which are on the cutting-edge frontier of social movement advertising and marketing research as a subfield of international management, all offering multidisciplinary perspectives firmly grounded in solid applied social science research and quantitative and qualitative methodologies. The marketing and advertising landscape has radically altered, and social movement marketing has made a front door entrance onto the stage powered by the full range of information and communication technologies. In a very tangible way, the marketing model in the global economy is gradually merging toward a form of what might be called cultural movement marketing which mobilizes heterogeneous, border-crossing populations through various platforms, and modalities which are responsive not only of the product mix and needs but also that of the consumer, society, and the global cultural model currently evolving. Conceptualized some 20 years ago, movement marketing and advertising was the brainchild of Scott Goodson, though older in its product-specific marketing

    DOI: 10.1057/9781137492265.0004

approaches. One can recall how the 1960s espoused the eco-conscious "small is the new big" (or "small is beautiful") notion and paired it with the counterculture of the day and age then.

There is naturally no lack of sociocultural movements today ranging from environmentalism to Occupy Wall Street. For a global business firm evolving global brands, knowing how to harness these movements, and how to support them appropriately to benefit the underlying society and culture, also has implications for the bottom line and the product's image and diffusion. Capturing a rising cultural idea and harnessing into the corporate culture of a family of products requires the mastery of social media methodologies. It requires new ways of phrasing foundational research questions responsive to this revolution in marketing and advertising. The challenge to what has been termed "push marketing" is clear and companies unable to adjust their marketing strategy suffer the consequence of market share loss magnified by the global size of their actual and potential market losses. The existence of a global network implicit in movement marketing demands that global audiences be understood in their similarities and differentiation along lines of consumer behavior and cultural value preferences. Social movements often find their point of departure in opposition to a trend, a system, a set of ideas or practices, which is challenged by a minority of early adopters of new paradigms to address sociopolitical issue configurations. In a very tangible way, social movements disturb equilibria and status quo; they unsettle audiences exposed to the new paradigm. Global movement marketing is not so much about selling products but rather understanding the value systems of various segments and populations, joining into a global ongoing conversation often challenging prevailing consensus. It requires a deep understanding of a society's fiber and a rapid harnessing of big data and other finer-grained techniques to forecast new trends and challenges.

This volume provides unique perspectives on global topics addressing in their varied foci the thematic confluence in advertising and marketing science. The first chapter on lipophilia and lipophobia illustrates tellingly how the concept of beauty and weight have become a central preoccupation of marketing in affluent societies in striking contrast to more tradition-bound societies. The second chapter focuses on creative hard-sell and soft-sell advertising appeals and highlights their relative advertising effectiveness taking gender into perspective. Do females like soft-sell more than hard-sell; or are hard-sell appeals targeting male

DOI: 10.1057/9781137492265.0004

audiences worldwide, are certain questions that this chapter seeks to answer. The chapter explores creative advertising campaigns and how advertising agencies can leverage a deep cross-cultural understanding in adjusting messages and strategies to various subcultures. The third chapter focuses on polysemy (or the diversity of meanings attributing to a single sign) in advertising messages and the impact of age differences on message processing. The fourth chapter bears on the notion of luxury goods marketing, the effect of country of origin, and the notion of "Made in France," and hence offers deep insights on product differentiation in the globalized market for luxury branded products. The fifth chapter of this special issue deals with brand diffusion and naming approaches as a corporation creates brand equity. The sixth chapter considers various mediums of advertising in commercials with particular reference to "tropes" used in figurative language and the appropriate interpretation by the target audience(s). The seventh chapter tests the concept of cultural stereotypes focusing on the African-American population and considers the impacts of advertising stereotypes on this population. Finally, the eighth chapter addresses the use and value of social networks in the changing landscape of global advertising and how companies have incorporated it into changing business models.

All in all this set of exploratory papers on challenging research topics goes a long way in opening new research vistas and buttressing the emerging paradigm around global social movement marketing.

Note

1   John R. McIntyre is Professor of Management and International Affairs in the Scheller College of Business at the Georgia Institute of Technology, Atlanta, Georgia, USA. He is also the founder of the Georgia Tech Center for International Business Education and Research now entering its 21st year of operations and dedicated to promoting research, education, and outreach in the cognate fields of international business.

DOI: 10.1057/9781137492265.0004

Series Editor

Anshu Saxena Arora, Ph.D., PMP is the Director of "Global Logistics and International Business Education Research (G-LIBER)" Center of Excellence and Associate Professor of Marketing in the College of Business Administration, Savannah State University, Savannah, Georgia. She is a Certified Project Management Professional (PMP) from Project Management Institute (PMI), USA, and holds a Foundation Certificate in IT Service Management from Information Systems Examination Board (ISEB), UK. Arora has been a visiting professor at ISC Paris Business School in France, University of California, Davis, and Thunderbird School of Global Management, Glendale, Arizona. Arora was awarded Ph.D. in Consumer Navigation Behavior in Hypermedia CMEs from the Indian Institute of Technology, Delhi, India. She has more than a decade of industrial and academic experience. She was the 2014 academic program chair for the Academy of International Business—Southeast (AIB-SE) conference held in Miami during October 23–25, 2014 (http://www.aibse.org/2014-annual-conference/2014-call-for-papers/). Her research interests and expertise include marketing analytics, stereotypical advertising polysemy, consumer behavior, ambient advertising, social media strategy mix and social media measurement, innovative experiential learning models in marketing and logistics/supply chain management, and relational supply chain strategy relationships.

Guest Editor

Sabine Bacouël-Jentjens, Ph.D., is Professor of Management at ISC Paris Business School in France. She is the Head of the "International Business & Management" Master Program. Sabine has been a visiting professor at various institutions in France (Ecole Nationale d'Administration ENA in Strasburg, Rouen Business School in Rouen, ICN Business School in Nancy, and ESCE in Paris), at Kozminski University in Warsaw, Poland, and at Bern University of Applied Sciences in Switzerland. Sabine holds a Master's in Finance and a Ph.D. in the area of cross-cultural human resource management, awarded from Trier University in Germany. In addition to research and teaching, she has more than a decade of practical experience in the financial services sector, working in both specialist and management positions for the Dresdner Bank and later Allianz Group in Germany. For both groups, she coauthored research work on European pension fund markets. Her current research interests and expertise focus on cross-cultural issues in various areas including HRM, organizational behavior, marketing, and diversity. She was the co-organizer for the colloquium "HRM in Asia—Distinctiveness of Asian Human Resource Management" held in Paris, France, from September 18 to 19, 2014 (http://www.hrminasia2014.iscparis.com).

DOI: 10.1057/9781137492265.0006

List of Contributors

Arora, Amit is Assistant Professor of Logistics and Supply Chain Management at Savannah State University.

Arora, Anshu Saxena is the Director of "Global Logistics and International Business Education Research (G-LIBER)" Center of Excellence and Associate Professor of Marketing in the College of Business Administration, Savannah State University.

Bacouel, Anne-Sophie is a student at the International School of Saint-Germain-en-Laye in France and recently experienced the Pennsylvania School for Global Entrepreneurship at Lehigh University.

Bacouël-Jentjens, Sabine is Professor of Management and Head of the master program "International Business & Management" at ISC Paris Business School in France.

Billinger, Eric is a 2013 graduate (BBA Computer Information System with minor in Global Logistics and International Business) from Savannah State University. He currently works as an officer at the US Air Force Georgia Air National Guard.

Bradford, Shalonda is the Associate Director of "Global Logistics and International Business Education Research (G-LIBER)," Center of Excellence and Lecturer of Management in the College of Business Administration, Savannah State University.

Brown, Ulysses J. III, is the Professor of Management in the College of Business Administration, Savannah State University.

Chasteen, William is a 2011 BBA Marketing graduate from Savannah State University, and is currently working as the Director of Advertising and Business Development at DGCpartners LLC.

Curry, Grace is a 2012 MBA graduate from Savannah State University. She has a Bachelor of Arts degree in Theatre from University of Georgia. Currently, Grace is the Assistant Director of WHCJ 90.3 FM at Savannah State University.

Gordon, Jamin is a BBA Marketing 2012 graduate from Savannah State University and currently she is a sales agent at GEICO in Macon, Georgia. She hopes to enter into the US Navy as an officer in the near future.

Harris, April MBA, CPC is a 2011 MBA graduate from Savannah State University. She received her undergraduate degree in Healthcare Administration, at Armstrong Atlantic State University. She is currently a Senior Healthcare Consultant for large hospitals and Physician Group Practices (including UCSD—San Diego, and Lucille Packard Children's Hospital at Stanford University).

Hudson, John is a 2012 BBA Marketing graduate from Savannah State University, and is currently employed by Microsoft Corporation where he serves on their marketing team working closely with resellers in a B2B format.

Leseane, Reginald is the Associate Dean and Associate Professor of Computer Information Systems at Savannah State University.

Lisa Yount, Ph.D., is Associate Professor of Philosophy and the Director of Savannah State University's Quality Enhancement Plan (QEP), "The Write Attitude: Enhancing Student Learning by Fostering Positive Attitudes toward Writing."

Loussaief, Leila is Professor of Marketing at ISC Paris Business School in France.

Rebufet, Manon recently graduated from ISC Paris Business School in France.

Wu, Jun is the Co-Director of "Global Logistics and International Business Education Research (G-LIBER)" Center of Excellence and Assistant Professor of Management in the College of Business Administration, Savannah State University.

DOI: 10.1057/9781137492265.0007

1

From Lipophilia to Lipophobia: The Role of Moral Entrepreneurs

Anne-Sophie Bacouël and Sabine Bacouël-Jentjens

▶

Abstract: *In the last decades, in most developed countries, fat has progressively been banished from both our plates and our bodies. Lipophobia is now growing in affluent societies, in striking contrast to traditional societies, where lipophilia prevails. In the last 30 years scientific, medical, and public health interest in obesity has skyrocketed. Increasingly the term "epidemic" is being used in the media to describe the current prevalence of corpulence in modern societies. To understand the phenomenon of increasing lipophobia and related issues, this paper focuses on how the standards toward fat evolved and on how moral entrepreneurs impact the perception of fat in Western societies via the use of media.*

Keywords: lipophilia; lipophobia; media; moral entrepreneurs

Arora, Anshu Saxena and Sabine Bacouël-Jentjens. *Advertising Confluence: Transitioning Marketing Communications into Social Movements.* New York: Palgrave Macmillan, 2015. DOI: 10.1057/9781137492265.0008.

Introduction

In the 1980s, the French Prime Minister Jacques Chirac revealed that he always perceived his lean physical appearance as a handicap in his political career. According to him, the voters always preferred the "chubby" politician (Fischler, 1987). This assertion is confirmed by empirical data collected from several countries, providing evidence that people with a more corpulent appearance were generally perceived as having a more amiable attitude and more open to communication and to empathy than people having a lean appearance (Fischler, 1987). Three decades later, however, France's current president, François Hollande, restrained to lose weight during his election campaign to qualify for the French presidentials (Grangeard, 2012). Therefore, the image of the body and the perception of weight seem to have changed, at least in France. However, when we look beyond borders, we notice that in other countries, the body mass does not influence the image of a politician in the same way. The current German government, for example, is more corpulent compared to the French. The image of corpulence thus seems to vary according to countries and cultures. However, the topic of obesity has gained importance in public discussion to the point of speaking about a worldwide epidemic.

According to the World Health Organization (2014), worldwide obesity has nearly doubled since 1980. In 2008, more than 1.4 billion adults were overweight and 500 million of these were obese (WHO, 2014). Obesity particularly affects contemporary societies in the developed world, and these societies seem to be turning lipophobic, that is, to be developing a marked aversion to fat. A corpulent body increasingly tends to be regarded as unaesthetic and unhealthy, while a lean body is apparently considered as a goal which is worth effort and cost (Fischler, 1992). The progression of lipophobia can be observed on three fronts: medicine and public health, fashion and corporal aesthetics (body image), and finally food consumption and eating habits.

To understand the current discussion about obesity and growing lipophobia, particularly in Western societies, our research concentrates on the perception of corpulence over time and strives to answer the following questions:

—How did the standards toward fat evolve in societies?
—Who are the moral entrepreneurs impacting the perception of fat in Western societies?
—How do moral entrepreneurs use media in the context of obesity?

DOI: 10.1057/9781137492265.0008

First, we shortly describe the evolution of fat perception over centuries and across cultures. Second, we analyze the factors leading to contemporary societies becoming increasingly lipophobic. In this context we will try to elaborate the influence of moral entrepreneurs such as the fashion, pharmaceutical, and food industry on obesity perception and their use of media to push forward their respective interests.

Lipophilic and lipophobic societies over the centuries

Fat has not always been a plague in the eyes of men; in fact it was considered as an ally in difficult times. It seems that in prehistoric societies, excessively corpulent mothers did not displease, as numerous statuettes such as the Venus of Willendorf testify. On the contrary, they represented fertility (Fischler, 1990: 342). While corpulence was valued in prehistoric societies, thinness was deprecated, representing exposure to the cold, disease, and famine (Ky et al., 1996). Under the Roman Empire fat was praised alike. Banquets were very frequently celebrated by the patricians, the elite of the Roman society, following the example given by the Roman emperors. Corpulence was a sign of wealth, attracting respect and authority (Ky et al., 1996). In medieval times, a reserve of fat was essential to survive in periods of famine or epidemics. But fat was also a symbol of pleasure and power reserved to the Lords (Ky et al., 1996). Later, during the Renaissance, the likeable women possessed full breasts, fleshy arms, a roundish chin, and a fat and round bust (Ky et al., 1996). This vision of the ideal body is illustrated by the Rubens paintings, where corpulent women are predominantly represented.

Today, in many societies different from the western ones, fat is often still positively considered, or at least was, until the western culture had its influence. Generally, African ideals of beauty are closer to stoutness than to thinness. Corpulence is valued, because it represents powerful position, social success, as well as health and fertility. Since the epidemic of AIDS, thin bodies are automatically linked to the disease. In Niger, girls take medications to increase their appetite, while in Mauritania they are fed in great quantities with sweet goat cream (Cohen et al., 2010; Effiong, 2013). In India, fat has been for a long time a symbol of success: corpulent people possessed enough money to afford food in abundance, to avoid manual labor, and to be loved and cherished by their peers. Stoutness was necessarily bound with happiness. Sridevi, the

DOI: 10.1057/9781137492265.0008

key Indian actress of the 1980s, had many curves and was nicknamed "Thunder Thighs" in reference to her voluminous thighs. Nowadays, it is the middle class that is increasingly becoming obese, thereby changing the image of obesity from prosperity and beauty to epidemic (Ranjani, 2011). In Tahiti, until the end of the 19th century, corpulence was the sign of upper-class membership. Even though the right of fattening in upper society is not practiced nowadays, Tahitians find corpulent people more attractive. The valuation of corpulence is a phenomenon still present in Tahiti, in spite of the strong influence of the thinness cult of western societies, communicated through the media (Prentice, 2006; Serra-Mallol, 2008).

In contrast, certain civilizations in the past can be described as lipophobic. In ancient Egypt, for instance, thinness was a fashion. Many ointments that refined the body tissue or eliminated weight were developed, and women were advised to avoid births too close together. Egyptians regularly practiced intestinal cleansing, intended to avoid obesity (Ky et al., 1996). In ancient Greece, beauty was mostly defined by symmetry with bulging muscles and athletic members. Being overweight was considered redundant and as a sign of decay of the body. Sports were very important to the Greeks. Even old Socrates invested in sport "to reduce his belly sticking out the right measure" (Ky et al., 1996). Baths in cold water were preferred because they were supposed to tone muscles and help avoid a protruding belly (Ky et al., 1996). One can also notice a certain food sobriety: the Greeks ate dried fruit, olives, and fish and avoided meat and large meals. In the 19th century, pale and thin women represented a certain ideal of beauty. Morbid femininity became fashion as Alexandre Dumas' "Lady of the Camellias": sunken eyes, hollow cheeks, thin body, and slender chest (Ky et al., 1996).

We were able to observe that the vision of and attitude toward fat have changed through the centuries, but also according to the cultural spheres. According to Sobal (2001), a person's cultural context is likely to be the most powerful influence on eating patterns, activity levels, and, therefore, body weight. Depending on the historical and geographical context, lipophilia is related to a need to survive, an image of good health, fertility, or the demonstration of wealth and power. In today's abundant societies, these values do not need to be demonstrated anymore by body shape. As a matter of fact, health, wealth, and power in those societies are nowadays more frequently symbolized by the ability to take care of one's body.

DOI: 10.1057/9781137492265.0008

How have standards toward fat changed?—the role of moral entrepreneurs

One may wonder how the views of society have changed so fundamentally from praising to cursing fat. The progression of lipophobia can be observed on three fronts: fashion and corporal aesthetics (body image), food consumption and eating habits, and medicine and public health. In each of these spheres, the so-called moral entrepreneurs set and push forward new standards, which are followed by the masses, and sanction those who do not or cannot respect these norms.

The objective existence of an obviously harmful condition such as obesity does not, by itself, constitute a social problem (Becker, 1966). Social problems may be looked at as constructed phenomena. In other words, what constitutes a problem is the concern that segments of the public express about a given condition. Definitions of social problems are produced by specific cultural circumstances, groups and categories, social structures and societies, historical eras, individuals, and/or classes (Goode & Ben-Yehuda, 1994).

Becker (1963; 1985) distinguishes two types of "moral entrepreneurs": those who create new standards and those who enforce them. The creator of standards is not satisfied with current laws or a certain type of behavior and considers them as personally offensive. The creators can be politicians, do-gooders, or activists who push for a given cause which might lead to a "crusade for moral reform" in order to obtain a change, for instance in legislation. This crusade can generate a moral panic, where reactions to a certain condition are out of proportion to the real and present danger that a given threat poses to the society. The notion of an obesity epidemic can be identified as a moral panic. In response to this exaggerated concern, deviant stereotypes which are said to be at the source of the threat, are created and identified as an official enemy. The crusade can succeed and lead to the creation of a new law or globally accepted norm, or fail and lead to the dissolution of the group of moral entrepreneurs or its reconversion (Goode & Ben-Yehuda, 1994). But once the moral reform is successful, its continuance must be ensured. It is the second type of moral entrepreneurs who are responsible for enforcing standards. These can be, for example, specially created institutions to sanction any breach of the law or norm (Becker, 1985). The most widely used perspective on moral panics has been the interest group approach. In this perspective, professional associations, media and other groups,

DOI: 10.1057/9781137492265.0008

and organizations are able to engage in collective action to generate and sustain moral panics which result in an increase of their wealth (Goode & Ben-Yehuda, 1994).

An important instigator of today's lipophobic standards was the US insurance industry. At the end of the 19th century, a new flourishing market for life insurances was born in the United States. In 1890, New York Life, an insurance company, searched for health indicators to assess the risk factors for each client in a better way. By analyzing statistics, the company realized that there was a correlation between premature death and weight of the insured. In 1942, the Metropolitan Life Insurance Company provided a table of ideal weights (Fischler, 2004), defining overweight as 10 per cent above the ideal body weight and obesity as 20–30 per cent higher than the ideal. According to Metropolitan, the mortality rate of obese men was 70 per cent and for women 61 per cent higher compared to people with "normal" weight (Fischler, 1990). These studies quickly became the basis of insurance companies to encourage their customers to lose weight. Later, it was proven that the statistics were misleading as most weights were self-reported by the policyholders and were not rechecked. In addition, the tables did not take the aging process and related weight gain into account: the table stated the ideal weight for 25-year-old individuals only. However, the elderly could not achieve the same weight due to changing conditions. Nevertheless, the US insurance lobby impacted public opinion and vilified obesity (Fischler, 1990). This triggered lipophobia in a way that it is nowadays perceived. For the insurance companies, the introduction of new weight standards generated higher premiums as a response to a supposedly higher risk. In the following section, we will discuss the role of medicine and public health sector, the body image industry (fashion and corporal aesthetics), and finally the food industry as moral entrepreneurs and discuss their actions in the light of the group interest approach. We will see that media play an important role for moral entrepreneurs to generate and sustain moral panic.

Boero's (2007) analysis of articles, published in the New York Times over a decade, shows that the term "epidemic" is increasingly being used not only in the media but also in medical journals and public health policy literature, when describing the current prevalence of corpulence in North America. Newspapers and magazines are filled with discussions of obesity and the health problems and associated risks. Simultaneously, the same media offer a vast array of advertising

DOI: 10.1057/9781137492265.0008

promoting ideal body shape and the appropriate products to achieve or maintain this condition.

Medicine and sciences

Doctors and obesity researchers are the fundamental moral entrepreneurs. They have the authority and their statements, made over the media, often influence the public. In 1998, due to the influence of these moral entrepreneurs, the US government decided to lower the threshold at which the individual is regarded overweight, from a body mass index of 27 down to 25. Thus, 25 million Americans, who were still in the normal weight category, became overweight overnight resulting in the perception of an obesity epidemic (Warren & Smalley, 2013).

Up until the last decades of the 20th century, moderate corpulence was considered attractive and healthy in most modern societies. A reasonably corpulent figure indicated good body management, and corpulence evoked sound financial assets (Schwartz, 1986; Seid, 1989). This lipophilic view of fat seems to have then been shared by most members of the medical profession (Schwartz, 1986). After World War II, the medical profession, influenced by the new insurance standards, took up an increasingly lipophobic stance. Corpulence came to be considered not only as an individual problem but also as a collective one, even a social one. Overweight and obesity were displayed as the consequences of overeating and unhealthy diets in a plethoric society. Obesity came to be regarded as one of the major factors in many modern pathologies, particularly coronary heart disease and diabetes (Prentice, 2006).

Today, a significant amount of research is published about obesity. However, many, if not most, of the obesity researchers are prominent consultants of the slimming, food, and pharmaceutical industry, and/or conduct research for these industries (Shell, 2002). "Some of the world's most prominent obesity experts, with backing from the drug industry and medical societies, defined obesity as a stand-alone 'disease' that caused premature death and needed to be treated with drugs" (Kelleher, 2005). By making obesity a disease, these experts have helped create a billion-dollar pharmaceutical, diet, and low-calorie food market.

The United States is most affected by obesity problems. Therefore, US organizations such as the American Obesity Association (AOA), the North American Association for the Study of Obesity (NAASO), and

DOI: 10.1057/9781137492265.0008

the Centers Obesity Research and Education are most prominent in the area of obesity research. It is often ignored that these organizations are funded by the food, pharmaceutical, and diet industries. All three associations have boardmembers of the related industry representatives. As the Center for Consumer Freedom (2005: 135) stated, AOA's board included the chief scientific officer of Weight Watchers, and a former senior medical director of Novartis. In 1996, NAASO's board consisted of representatives from contributing companies such as Eli Lilly, Roche, Procter & Gamble Co., Slimfast Foods, and Wyeth-Ayerst Laboratories (The Center for Consumer Freedom, 2005). On June 18, 2013, the American Medical Society recognized obesity as a disease which was considered a major victory for these associations. Following this statement, a law was proposed to further expand the support for treatments against obesity through Medicare, opening a billion-dollar market for the pharmaceutical industry.

The body image industry—fashion, cosmetics, and accessories

Not only the weight but also the shape of the ideal female body has changed considerably over time. For centuries, numerous contraptions forced women's bodies into the desired form. Since the beginning of this century, the preferred shape for the female body has evolved, in particular in North America, from the so-called hourglass model (thin waist, ample hips, and breasts) to the "tubular" muscular model, in which the contrast between waist, hips, and bosom is less marked. This evolution is exemplified in magazine illustrations between 1900 and 1981 or in Playboy centerfold playmates from 1960 to 1980 (Garner et al., 1980; Silverstein et al., 1986). Muscles, formerly a purely masculine feature, became increasingly desirable for women. This is particularly conspicuous in the United States, with the spread of exercise and sports among women starting in the 1970s and 1980s (Fischler, 1992; 2004). From the 1960s onward, a large part of the population in western societies was able to afford basic fashion-related products such as cosmetics, prêt-à-porter, and accessories. Industrialization contributed significantly to the improvement of textile availability and cosmetics. In the same time, American movie stars, models, beauty queens, and singers helped to spread the aesthetic ideal of the modern woman, by directing women to

DOI: 10.1057/9781137492265.0008

the glorification of a slim body (Fischler, 1990; Lipovetsky, 1997). In the Europe of the late 1960s, the race for thinness in the fashion world was launched by the model Twiggy (Apfeldorfer, 2006). Highly publicized by advertising and the media, Twiggy embodied a new model of beauty. Earlier the talent of a fashion designer was measured by his or her ability to adjust the garment to the body of his client; however, today it is rather his or her ability to create a garment that is valued. This trend gradually introduced the idea that the body must comply to the garment (Bourque, 2004: 60). A recent example is the declaration of the US-American fashion company Abercrombie & Fitch, in May 2013, that they did not want their clothes being worn by obese clients anymore. Larger sizes for plus-sized women were eliminated (Nouvel Observateur, 2013). Thinness as a beauty norm is now a quasi-"global" standard prevalent in all developed countries; the body now obeys "international standards" (Amadieu, 2002). Nevertheless, existing norms become increasingly criticized by new moral entrepreneurs claiming a change in promoting excessive thinness. The participation of extremely thin models in international fashion parades was forbidden in several European fashion capitals (such as Madrid or Rome) in the past years. As an example, Victoria's Secret is a lingerie brand that typically uses young mannequins with a perfectly sculpted body. Since 2001, Victoria's Secret's annual broadcast television show has attracted protests from US lobby groups, such as the Parents Television Council, the National Organization for Women, and the American Decency Association claiming that their models were a bad example of excessive thinness.

Other companies within the fashion-related cosmetics industry have taken advantage of these trends. Unilever's brand Dove addressed a more corpulent female clientele by mocking Victoria's Secret's advertising, by positively exposing strong built and curved women in underwear. The Swedish fashion giant H&M balanced its advertising efforts by promoting its garments simultaneously by more corpulent models such as Jennie Runk who is recently advertising H&M's swimsuits collection.

The food industry—a double-tracked interest

In the last 20 years, new products have appeared in the food industry and trends have accelerated, with the proliferation of new low-fat products and diet foods. The consumption of butter and red meat has,

DOI: 10.1057/9781137492265.0008

for instance, declined in the United States and France (Fischler, 1990) and new slimming products have been developed. The food industry profits in a double way from lipophobic trends. First, this industry is at the origin of producing high-calorie food such as sodas, cakes, and ready-made meals such as pizza, promoting as a moral entrepreneur new eating habits through fast-food restaurants (Lapostolle et al., 2013) and the distribution of ready-made meals. The quantities of sugar incorporated into processed foods and sugary drinks have increased sharply. Consumption of those products has also increased notably due to changing cooking and eating habits (less time sacrificed to cooking at home) and increased advertising of the benefits of industrially processed food. Simultaneously, the same industry promotes light products or weight-reducing products by either praising the maintenance of a thin body or promising the achievement of this desirable condition, reinforcing therefore the trend of lipophobia.

Food may be represented as delicious and healthy, avoiding any negative effects on the body mass as suggested in Kellogg's Special cereal advertising. Other companies clearly display lipophobic positions such as the advertising for Brazil's Fit Light Yogurt parodying the legendary scene from the movie "Seven Year Itch" with Marilyn Monroe with her dress lifted by the blast of an air vent. Instead of the American star, a very stout young woman is observed telling the customers to "Forget it. Men's preferences never change." This advertisement clearly displays its lipophobic positioning for low-fat yogurt. The Brazilian context devoted to the culture of athletic body probably partly explains the hardness of the message against the obese. Finally, in an ad for Slim Fast a wedding cake is displayed on which the married couple is not in place because the bride broke into the cake. The slogan is clear: "Do you need to lose a little weight before your marriage?" The message, although in the tone of humor, is clearly lipophobic.

Conclusion

We have previously shown that fat has not always been abhorred and, in fact, was actually very popular in the past or in traditional societies. However, moral entrepreneurs in western societies have, over time, impacted the standards of fat perception, generating an evolution from praise to curse. These moral entrepreneurs in particular represent the

DOI: 10.1057/9781137492265.0008

pharmaceutical, fashion, and food industry. Interest-orientated, they use the creation of a moral panic of an obesity epidemic to open new markets for their products. Industries such as the food industry even play a double role as moral entrepreneur, on the one hand, by promoting modern and fast, high-calorie food products; and on the other hand, by demonizing the eventual obesity outcomes of these promoted eating habits and offering low-calorie products to control obesity. The use of media and advertising reinforces the moral entrepreneurs' actions. The theory of moral entrepreneurs may explain the evolution of lipophobia, but cannot completely explain the objective increase of obesity in many societies. Socioeconomic status, changing lifestyles, new working patterns, and technological advancements also have an impact on eating habits and weight gain which have to be analyzed to understand a holistic picture about the phenomenon of obesity and lipophobia.

References

Amadieu, J.-F. (2002). *Le Poids des apparences: Beauté, amour et gloire.* Éditons Odile Jacob.

Apfeldorfer, G. (2006). *Maigrir, c'est fou !* Paris: Odile Jacob, coll. Pratique.

Becker, H. S. (1963). *Outsiders: Studies in the Sociology of Deviance.* New York: Fee.

Becker, H. S. (1966). *Social Problems: A Modern Approach.* New York: Wiley.

Becker, H. S. (1985). *Outsiders. Études de sociologie de la déviance.* Éditions Métailié.

Boero, N. (2007). All the News that's Fat to Print: The American "Obesity Epidemic" and the Media. *Qualitative Sociology*, 30, 41–60.

Bourque, D. (2004). *Á 10 kilo du bonheur. L'obsession de la minceur.* Ses causes. Ses effets. Comment s'en sortir. 2ème Édition. Québec: Les éditions de l'homme.

Cohen, E., Chapuis-Lucciani, N., Pasquet, P., Guye, L., & Boëtsch, G. (2010). *L'image du corps chez les Sénégalais: Application à l'étude de l'obésité dans le contexte de la transition des modes de vie.* L'anthropologie du vivant: objets et méthodes. 52–57.

Effiong, P. U. (2013). *Nigerian "Fattening" Rooms: Reinventing the total Woman,* http://www.philip-effiong.com/Fattening-Rooms.pdf , Accessed November 16, 2014.

DOI: 10.1057/9781137492265.0008

Fischler, C. (1987). Le symbolique du gros. *Communications*, 46, 255–278.

Fischler, C. (1990). *L'Homnivore. Le goût, la cuisine et le corps.* Éditions Odile Jacob.

Fischler, C. (1992). From Lipophilia to Lipophobia. Changing Attitudes towards Fat: ASocio-Historical Approach. In D. J. Mela (ed.), *Dietary Fats Determinants of Preference, Selection and Consumption.* London, New York: Elsevier Applied Sciences, pp. 103–115.

Fischler, C. (2004). Le Gras. Le Nouvel Observateur Hors-Série « Mythologies d'aujourd'hui. 36–37.

Garner, D. M., Garfinkel, P. E., Schwartz, D., & Thompson, M. (1980). Cultural Expectations of Thinness in Women. *Psychological Reports,* 47, 483–491.

Goode, E., & Ben-Yehuda, N. (1994). Moral Panics: Culture, Politics and Social Constructions. *Annual Review of Sociology,* 20(1), 149–173.

Grangeard, C. (2012). *Comprendre l'obésité. Une question de personne, un problème de société.* Paris: Albin Michel.

Kelleher, S. (2005). Rush toward a New Weight-loss Drugs Tramples Patients' Health. The Seattle Times. June 27, 2005. http://seattletimes.com/html/health/sick2.html accessed May 19, 2014.

Ky, T., Didou-Manet, M., & Robert, H. (1996). *Mince ou grosse. Histoire du corps idéal.* Paris: Académique Perrin.

Lapostolle, F., Alhéritière, A., Montois, S., Galinski, M. & Tazarourte, K. (2013). Worldwide Relation between the Number of McDonald's Restaurants and the Prevalence of Obesity. *Journal of Internal Medicine.* 274 (6), 610–611.

Lipovetsky, G. (1997). *La troisième femme.* Paris: Gallimard, coll. Folio essais.

Nouvel Observateur (2013). Abercrombie & Fitsch, la marquee des gens beaux, minces et riches. http://rue89.nouvelobs.com/2013/05/14/abercrombie-fitch-marque-gens-beaux-minces-riches-242324 accessed May 20, 2014.

Prentice, A. M. (2006). The Emerging Epidemic of Obesity in Developing Countries. *International Journal of Epidemiology,* 35, 93–99.

Ranjani, I. M. (2011). The Rise and Fall of Fat in India. *The New York Times,* September 14, 2011.

Schwartz, H. (1986). *Never Satisfied. A Cultural History of Diets, Fantasies and Fat.* New York: The Free Press.

Seid, R. P. (1989). *Never Too Thin,* New York: Prentice Hall.

DOI: 10.1057/9781137492265.0008

Serra-Mallol, C. (2008). Bien manger, c'est manger beaucoup: comportements alimentaires et représentations corporelles à Tahiti. *Sciences Sociales et Santé*, 26(4), 81–112.

Shell, E. R. (2002) *The Hungry Gene. The Science of Fat and the Future of Thin.* New York: Atlantic Monthly Press.

Silverstein, B., Peterson, B., & Perdue, L. (1986). Some Correlates of the Thin Standard of Bodily Attractiveness for Women. *International Journal of Eating Disorders*, 5(5), 895–905.

Sobal, J. (2001). Social and Cultural Influences on Obesity. In P. Björntorp (ed.), *International Textbook of Obesity*. Chichester: John Wiley & Sons, pp. 305–318.

The Center for Consumer Freedom (2005). *The Epidemic of Obesity Myths*. Washington, DC: The Center for Consumer Freedom.

Warren, J. C., & Smalley, K. B. (2013). Always the Fat Kid: The Truth about the Enduring Effects of Childhood Obesity. New York: Palgrave Macmillan.

WHO—World Health Organization (2014). Obesity and Overweight. Fact sheet No 311. Reviewed May 2014. www.who.int/mediacentre/factsheets/fs311/en/ accessed May 20, 2014.

DOI: 10.1057/9781137492265.0008

2
Creative Advertising Appeals on Global Cultural Spectrum

John Hudson and Anshu Saxena Arora

Abstract: *The research focuses on consumer advertising appeals on a cross-cultural spectrum. It is imperative for advertising agencies to understand that each culture is not only different on a global cultural spectrum but also unique in different subcultures. The perceptions of advertising appeals are ever changing and this research study discusses the different appeals used to target consumers across the global cultural spectrum. This chapter proposes the AD Hard–Soft conceptual framework which focuses on attitudes toward the ad, brand and purchase intentions through the usage of hard- and soft-sell advertising appeals. The chapter uses qualitative research wherein different ads with varying advertising appeals were utilized and their findings are recorded. The differences between hard- and soft-sell are highlighted through this research.*

Keywords: advertising appeals; global cultural spectrum; hard-sell; sex appeals; soft-sell

Arora, Anshu Saxena and Sabine Bacouël-Jentjens. *Advertising Confluence: Transitioning Marketing Communications into Social Movements.* New York: Palgrave Macmillan, 2015. DOI: 10.1057/9781137492265.0009.

DOI: 10.1057/9781137492265.0009

Introduction and review

As globalization continues to develop at a fast pace, many consumers are being able to view advertisements of products from regions they could not view a few years ago. According to Kalliny & Gentry (2007), the diminishing of national boundaries has increased more than ever the selection of products and brand names from which customers can choose. Many of the top 100 brands have worldwide presence in more than 100 countries (Mueller, Okazaki, & Taylor, 2010).

Hard-sell refers to a more direct approach to selling while in contrast soft-sell approaches are more subtle and indirect (Okazaki, Mueller, & Taylor, 2010a). The approach is also viewed as the difference of video advertising between commercials (soft-sell) and infomercials (hard-sell).

In this research study, hard- and soft-sell approaches are compared and contrasted. The soft-sell approach is more suitable when it is based on image-oriented content that does not emphasize specific reasons to buy but rather conveys general association with the brand (Okazaki, Mueller, & Taylor, 2010a). This is why Japan, China, India, and other Eastern nations favorably use soft-sell approaches that will not offend consumers by using a direct aggressive approach. It is culturally offensive and even disrespectful to directly approach consumers with the benefits and features of a product or service without first luring them in with a favorable image, perhaps through sensitivity of emotions which are culturally significant and relevant. In contrast, the hard-sell approach is based on distinct and explicit content that emphasizes product advantages, performance (Okazaki, Mueller, & Taylor, 2010b), and the factual information may be mixed easily with soft-sell by way of imagery and animation.

In contrast to the many definitions that have been provided for hard- and soft-sell in the advertising literature, there is no common definition or specific device that can be used to measure either type of appeal.

The research goal is to compare and contrast the effectiveness of hard- and soft-sell approaches vis-à-vis different cultures. This research addresses the following questions:

—Why is soft-sell appeal more effective for brand awareness, while hard-sell is more effective to persuade a consumer to make an immediate purchase?

DOI: 10.1057/9781137492265.0009

—Why is culture the reason advertising appeals must differ to be effective in target markets of various geographic locations? and
—How are modern trends influencing people of different cultures to be more acceptant of advertising appeals that would otherwise be rejected?

The research proposes the AD Hard–Soft conceptual framework highlighting the attitudes toward the advertising, brand and purchase intentions with the usage of hard- and soft-sell advertising appeals.

Literature review

Okazaki, Mueller, & Taylor (2010b) note that the hard- and soft-sell advertising concepts have been researched and provided with definitions since 1911. Through intensive research, reviews, and discussions they "proposed that three fundamental dimensions underlie soft- and hard-sell appeals: feeling vs. thinking, implicit versus explicit, and image versus fact" (Okazaki, Mueller, & Taylor, 2010b). Soft-sell approaches that displayed images, beautiful pictures and scenery, and other indirect methods were less annoying and aggressive.

Chu, Gerstner, & Hess (1995) concluded that hard-sell approaches had a better chance of surviving in a more competitive environment, consumers are negatively affected, and sellers gain more from making their products better (to make features more appealing than competitors). In fact, telemarketers are taught not to use hard-sell approaches at all, but to simply use a script that detects interested consumers (Jolson, 1986). Soft-sell approaches may be more effective when selling products that provide pleasure, whereas technological and functional products and services sell best with a hard-sell approach that can promote the features and benefits. However, simply using a hard-sell approach may fail if good customer service and satisfaction are not provided for the consumer (Marr & Prendergast, 1990).

To further distinguish between hard- and soft-sell, "three primary dimensions of soft-sell appeals: feeling (creative, instinctive, imaginative, and abstract), implicitness (insinuation, appealing, subjective, and expressive), image (entertaining, interpretive, playful, and impression based)" were provided by Okazaki, Mueller, & Taylor (2010b). On the other hand, Okazaki, Mueller, & Taylor (2010a) stated that hard-sell

DOI: 10.1057/9781137492265.0009

appeals consist of three dimensions: thinking (rational, logical, analytic, factual, and concrete), explicitness (precise, explanation, convincing, persuasion, and instructive), and fact (educational, descriptive, realistic, informative, and evidence-based).

Bülbül & Menon (2010) provided distinctions of how hard-sell appeals are more concrete and may generate behavioral responses instantly. Their research suggested that hard-sell advertisements influence the consumer to make a decision immediately, but loyalty will not be established as it would through the feelings that are generated through soft-sell advertisements that produce emotions. Chandy, Tellis, Macinnis, & Thaivanich (2001) provide a framework for determining why certain appeals work better in different markets and cultures. Chinese commercials use more soft-sell approaches because it is not polite to be direct in the Chinese culture (Lin, 2001).

Most modern, Western nations use more hard-sell approaches, with the exception of Britain. Britain uses soft-sell approach widely and effectively due to the presence of multicultural diverse population, differences in the social–cultural contexts, advertising industry environment variances, and differences in philosophy and execution that may be controlled by government and political structure (Nevett, 1992).

Sexual appeals in advertising

Sexual appeals in advertising often are composed of a variety of execution elements, including visual elements (e.g., attractive models and nudity), suggestive verbal elements and music, or "scent-strip" advertising (Garcia & Yang, 2006). It can be stated that different regulations in different countries play a major role in what is advertised and what is not. "Such restrictions may also be applied to advertising codes in China, for our findings also indicated Chinese ads in both TV and magazine showed the lowest degrees of nudity across all countries" (Paek & Nelson, 2007). Due to China's strong regulations on nudity on television, the culture in China can be perceived as one that does not agree with the sexual appeals of advertising. Many advertisers would have to create a new campaign to target their product to a Chinese consumer if their product had any signs of sexual appeals in the advertisement.

A popular commercial from Axe Body Spray is advertised in many countries. The commercial starts by showing a man that turns into a

DOI: 10.1057/9781137492265.0009

chocolate figurine after dousing himself in Axe Dark Temptation body spray. While wandering the streets and through different areas of his city he is licked and at the end a woman takes a bite out of his butt. This commercial is considered very risqué in parts of the world such as India where this advertisement has been banned by the government. This is a very prime example of the importance of knowing your region and making sure your advertisements are adaptable.

Levi's advertisements use both soft- and hard-sell advertising appeals that target different cultures. In one of their hard-sell advertisement, everyone is fully clothed and there is a simple tagline. Another ad uses more of a sexual appeal by using a topless male actor and a female feeling on his genital area. When a small focus group was asked to select the best way to convey the message, the views were split 50 percent by 50 percent. Many of the students in the focus group felt the clothed models were more decent and more interesting. One student wrote, "Great message and tagline; it was not sexist or bias." Some female students felt that the shirtless model in the second ad was a lot better because they viewed the model as sexy. A female student wrote, "He's cute and it's a sexy ad that I would like to see my boyfriend in." It is safe to say that sexual appeals can be used and be effective but often if the message is conveyed correctly through words, it can be just as effective.

Brand and ad attitudes

Mitchell & Olson (1981) highlighted the major influence of the attitude toward the ad (A_{ad}) by demonstrating that the effect of visual and emotional elements on the attitude toward the brand (A_b) is mediated by A_{ad}. This theory assumes a direct link between A_{ad} and A_b and implies that a positive attitude toward the ad is directly carried over to a positive attitude toward the brand (Geuens & Pelsmacker, 1998). Research has concluded that ad evaluations were debilitated by negative affect and stimulated by positive affect (Goldberg & Gorn, 1987; Mitchell, 1986; Russo, Shah, & Park, 1994; Scrull, 1983).

Figure 2.1 illustrates the Dual Mediation Hypothesis model. This model has received most support as a means of representing the interrelationships between A_{ad}, brand and ad cognitions, A_b and PI (MacKenzie & Lutz, 1989; Brown & Stayman, 1992).

Figure 2.1 supports models of Okazaki, Mueller, & Taylor (2010a) in a way that there is no direct correlation between the dimensions and

FIGURE 2 .1 *Dual Mediation Hypothesis model*

the advertising appeals, but they can be used as ad-measurements and consequences. Common feelings and other characteristics may be apparent in certain types of appeals, but there has been no proof of how brand and ad attitudes, purchase intention, purchase initiators, and other factors are directly correlated as a result of certain ads displaying specific appeals.

Conceptual framework

Okazaki, Mueller, & Taylor (2010) provided with the models of hard- and soft-sell advertising appeals. Dual Mediation Hypothesis model elaborated on the relationships between ad and brand cognitions, and ad and brand attitudes, leading to purchase intentions. A model called AD Hard–Soft framework (Figure 2.2) is conceptualized, illustrating the hard- and soft-sell advertising appeals and their consequences on building ad and brand attitudes and purchase intentions. The model is created from the goals and objectives of a firm, which may actually determine which appeal is used, along with the cultural context of the firm/company.

The AD Hard–Soft model in Figure 2.2 illustrates the cause and effect relationship between the advertising appeals (hard- and soft-sell), attitudes (toward the advertisement and brand), and subsequently to purchase intentions.

Figure 2.2 illustrates our conceptual framework—"AD Hard–Soft" model depicting the drivers of hard- and soft-sell appeals and their consequences. We conceptualize a direct relationship of hard- and soft-sell advertising appeals with attitude toward the advertisement and attitude toward the brand, which further affect the purchase intentions.

DOI: 10.1057/9781137492265.0009

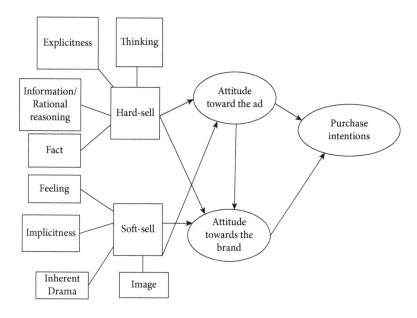

FIGURE 2.2   *AD hard–soft conceptual framework and drivers of hard- and soft-sell appeals*

Figure 2.2 shows four drivers for hard-sell advertising appeal—thinking, explicitness, informational/rational reasoning, and fact—and four drivers for soft-sell advertising appeal—feeling, implicitness, inherent drama, and image. These drivers lead to the attitude toward the ad, brand and purchase intentions.

Research methodology

A focus group research was conducted where a sample size of 70 undergraduate students at a Historically Black College University (HBCU) was selected for the purpose of the research study, out of which 45 were women. The group was divided into two focus groups of 35 students each. The study was confined to alcoholic and automobile ads. There are several reasons for choosing these categories—all subjects were old enough to drink legally and responsibly, and they had a common preference for cars/automobiles. Seven volumes of five business/fashion magazines and newspapers (Vanity Fair, Time, Cosmopolitan, Wall

DOI: 10.1057/9781137492265.0009

Street Journal, and People) were screened—the result was an initial set of 33 ads in three categories.

First qualitative stage: Thirty-three ads/stimuli were presented to a jury of 15 students in order to judge the degree of humor, warmth, and eroticism of each stimulus. The results of this qualitative stage were ordered category ranking of 33 stimuli—frequency counts were conducted and finally, eight stimuli were selected—two stimuli with the highest number of assignments to the "humorous" category, two warm, two erotic, and two nonemotional/neutral hard-sell stimuli. The hard-sell neutral stimulus was defined as the one often assigned as "not humorous," "not erotic," and "not warm").

Second qualitative stage: These eight stimuli were then presented to the two focus groups of 35 students each, in random order for each student. Randomization was used to avoid systematic measurement errors as a result of respondent wear-out. Since the population at a HBCU is homogenous with similar sociodemographic characteristics, only gender was included as a classification question. Thereafter, the findings were recorded for these focus groups and generalized for males versus females.

Research findings

After conducting the research, we obtained the results as shown in Appendix I. Women feel more cheerful than men when warm and soft-sell ads are conveyed and the opposite is true for erotic stimuli—men feel more cheerful than women when exposed to erotic ads (refer to Tables 2.1–2.4). Soft-sell emotional appeals of warmth, humor, and eroticism lead to more positive feelings than the nonemotional hard-sell appeals.

Brand interest and positive emotion and impression about the brand and an ad lead to positive purchase intention. Soft-sell strategies make ads more interesting and likeable leading to positive intentions to buy, while hard-sell strategies ignite more likeability but do not strike interest in the target audience.

Conclusion

The research study revisits the concepts of advertising appeals, especially hard- and soft-sell appeals, and explains how there is not one widely

DOI: 10.1057/9781137492265.0009

accepted definition for an appeal. However, the fundamental dimensions to measure these appeals are widely accepted, as depicted in Figures 1a and 1b. Our proposed AD Hard—Soft conceptual model may be accepted with new dimensions of information/rational reasoning dimension, inherent drama, and image, with theory and reasonable explanations. The information/rational reasoning dimension has been added because it is needed to explain the functional aspect of the hard-sell approach. Without information and reasoning, the functional perspective of the hard-sell approach is nonexistent in an advertising strategy. Likewise, the inherent drama dimension has been added to the soft-sell model because emotions, feelings, and the other dimensions that measure a soft-sell appeal do not exist if the advertising strategy cannot emphasize the benefits of purchasing a product or service.

Our research findings are significant with respect to the use of warmth, humor, and eroticism as soft-sell appeals and neutral stimulus as hard-sell appeal. The limitations of the study are that only print ads were used and analyzed, students alone were included, and existing products' ads were used. It may be argued that for new brands and new products, emotional soft-sell advertising appeals may be less suited and informational hard-sell appeals will work better. Future research may focus on the new added dimensions of hard- and soft-sell advertising appeal drivers.

Appendix I

TABLE 2.1   *Perceived level of warmth, eroticism, humor, and fear in ads (1=low, 7=high)*

Level of	Warmth	Eroticism	Humor	Fear	Neutral
Warmth	4.9	4.2	3.5	1.5	2.2
Eroticism	3.7	4.4	1.8	1.3	2.1
Humor	3.3	2.7	5.1	2.3	1.5
Fear	3.4	2.8	2.1	4.9	2.5

DOI: 10.1057/9781137492265.0009

TABLE 2.2 Correlation between ad-evoked feelings (1=strongest negative feeling; 7=strongest positive feeling)

Correlations

		Worried carefree	Depressed cheerful	Insulted honored	Indifferent interested	Irritated pleased	Regretful rejoicing
worried carefree	Pearson correlation	1	0.634**	0.553**	0.498**	0.620**	0.577**
	Sig. (1-tailed)		0.000	0.000	0.000	0.000	0.000
	Covariance	2.835	1.537	1.261	1.222	1.529	1.366
Depressed cheerful	Pearson correlation	0.634**	1	0.628**	0.536**	0.675**	0.712**
	Sig. (1-tailed)	0.000		0.000	0.000	0.000	0.000
	Covariance	1.537	2.076	1.225	1.125	1.425	1.440
Insulted honored	Pearson correlation	0.553**	0.628**	1	0.569**	0.620**	0.604**
	Sig. (1-tailed)	0.000	0.000		0.000	0.000	0.000
	Covariance	1.261	1.225	1.835	1.123	1.231	1.150
Indifferent interested	Pearson correlation	0.498**	0.536**	0.569**	1	0.616**	0.563**
	Sig. (1-tailed)	0.000	0.000	0.000		0.000	0.000
	Covariance	1.222	1.125	1.123	2.125	1.315	1.152
Irritated pleased	Pearson correlation	0.620**	0.675**	0.620**	0.616**	1	0.636**
	Sig. (1-tailed)	0.000	0.000	0.000	0.000		0.000
	Covariance	1.529	1.425	1.231	1.315	2.146	1.309
Regretful rejoicing	Pearson correlation	0.577**	0.712**	0.604**	0.563**	0.636**	1
	Sig. (1-tailed)	0.000	0.000	0.000	0.000	0.000	
	Covariance	1.366	1.440	1.150	1.152	1.309	1.973

Note: **Correlation is significant at the 0.01 level (1-tailed).

DOI: 10.1057/9781137492265.0009

TABLE 2.3   *Summary of exploratory factor analysis results for ad-evoked feelings*

	Rotated Factor Loadings				
	Cheerful (reverse coded)	Insulted	Irritated	Interested	Carefree (reverse coded)
• Pessimistic _____ hopeful	0.777	0.253	0.156	0.284	0.177
• Callous _____ affectionate	0.731	0.265	0.180	0.285	0.172
• Dubious _____ confident	0.662	0.258	0.335	0.229	0.236
• Bad _____ good	0.618	0.462	0.385	0.151	0.024
• Cautious _____ adventurous	0.549	0.353	0.339	−0.018	0.449
• Critical _____ accepting	0.458	0.376	0.394	0.125	0.455
• Insulted _____ honored	0.237	0.754	0.194	0.246	0.153
• Depressed _____ cheerful	0.670	0.282	0.206	0.317	0.293
• Regretful _____ rejoicing	0.368	0.668	0.187	0.219	0.253
• Sad _____ happy	0.423	0.607	0.461	0.100	0.139
• Irritated _____ pleased	0.252	0.224	0.585	0.339	0.224
Worried ___ carefree	0.258	0.326	0.284	0.141	0.784
Nervous ___ calm	0.304	0.260	0.764	0.201	0.269
• Unemotional __ sentimental	0.215	0.174	0.081	0.861	0.266
• Indifferent _____ interested	0.288	0.386	0.266	0.612	0.287
• Contemplative __ impulsive	0.214	0.265	0.287	0.205	0.807
Eigenvalues	3.32	3.27	2.46	1.75	1.60
% of variance	20.77	20.49	15.37	10.92	9.97
Cronbach alpha	0.92	0.84	0.80	0.82	0.82

Extraction method: Principal Component Analysis
Rotation method: Varimax with Kaiser Normalization

Rotation converged in seven iterations

KMO and Bartlett's test

Kaiser–Meyer–Olkin measure of sampling adequacy		0.967
Bartlett's test of sphericity	Approx. Chi-Square	19284.226
	Sig.	0.000

DOI: 10.1057/9781137492265.0009

TABLE 2.4   *Perceived level of warmth, eroticism, humor, and fear in ads (1=low, 7=high) for males and females*

Level of	Warmth	Eroticism	Humor	Fear	Neutral
Cheerful (Male)	3.5	4.1	3.5	2.5	4.2
Cheerful (Female)	3.9	3.2	3.9	1.5	3.2
Insulted (Male)	3.9	3.4	2.8	4.0	4.1
Insulted (Female)	3.7	4.4	3.8	4.3	3.9
Irritated (Male)	3.7	3.7	3.8	4.3	4.5
Irritated (Female)	3.3	3.9	3.5	3.8	4.1
Interested (Male)	3.8	4.5	3.6	3.9	3.5
Interested (Female)	3.7	4.0	3.4	4.3	2.8

Note: *Correlation is significant at the 0.05 level (1-tailed); **Correlation is significant at the 0.01 level (1-tailed).

References

Brown S. P., & Stayman D. M. (1992). Antecedents and Consequences of Attitude towards the Ad: A Meta-Analysis. *Journal of Consumer Research*, 19, 34–51.

Bülbül C., & Menon G. (2010). The Power of Emotional Appeals in Advertising. *Journal of Advertising Research*, 50 (2), 169–180.

Chandy R., Tellis G., Macinnis D., & Thaivanich P. (2001). What to Say When: Advertising Appeals in Evolving Markets. *Journal of Marketing Research (JMR)*, 38 (4), 399–414.

Chu W., Gerstner E., & Hess J. (1995). Costs and Benefits of Hard-Sell. *Journal of Marketing Research (JMR)*, 32(1), 97–102.

Garcia E., & Yang K. C. C. (2006). Consumer Responses to Sexual Appeals in Cross-Cultural Advertisements. *Journal of International Consumer Marketing*, 19(2), 23.

Geuens M., & de Pelsmacker P. (1998). Feelings Evoked by Warm, Erotic, Humorous or Non-Emotional Print Advertisements for Alcoholic Beverages. *Academy of Marketing Science Review*, 98(1).

Goldberg M. E., & Gorn G. J. (1987). Happy and Sad TV Programs: How They Affect Reactions to Commercials. *Journal of Consumer Research*, 387–403.

DOI: 10.1057/9781137492265.0009

Jolson M. (1986). Prospecting by Telephone Prenotification: An Application of the Foot-In-The-Door Technique. *Journal of Personal Selling & Sales Management*, 6(2), 39.

Kalliny M., & Gentry L. (2007). Cultural Values in Arab and American Television Advertising. *Journal of Current Issues and Research in Advertising*, 29, 17.

Lin C. (2001). Cultural Values Reflected in Chinese and American Television Advertising. *Journal of Advertising*, 30(4), 83–94.

Mackenzie S. B., & Lutz R. J. (1989). An Empirical Examination of the Structural Antecedents of Attitude towards the Ad in an Advertising Pretesting Context. *Journal of Marketing*, 53, 48–65.

Marr N., & Prendergast G. (1990). EFTPOS: The Perils of a Cost-Driven Venture. *Service Industries Journal*, 10(4), 748–758.

Mitchell A. A. (1986). The Effect of Verbal and Visual Components of Advertisements on Brand Attitudes and Attitude towards the Advertisement. *Journal of Consumer Research*, 12–23.

Mitchell A. A., & Olson J. C. (1981). Are Product Attribute Beliefs the Only Mediator of Advertising Effects on Brand Attitude? *Journal of Marketing Research*, 18, 318–332.

Mueller B., Okazaki S., & Taylor C. R. (2010). Global Consumer Culture Positioning: Testing Perceptions of Soft-Sell and Hard-Sell Advertising Appeals Between U.S. and Japanese Consumers. *Journal of International Marketing*, 18(2), 20–34.

Nevett T. (1992). Differences between American and British Television Advertising: Explanations and Implications. *Journal of Advertising*, 21(4), 61–71.

Okazaki S., Mueller B., & Taylor C. (2010a). Global Consumer Culture Positioning: Testing Perceptions of Soft-Sell and Hard-Sell Advertising Appeals between U.S. and Japanese Consumers. *Journal of International Marketing*, 18(2), 20–34.

Okazaki S., Mueller B., & Taylor C. (2010b). Measuring Soft-Sell Versus Hard-Sell Advertising Appeals. *Journal of Advertising*, 39(2), 5–20.

Paek H.-J., & Nelson M. (2007). A Cross-Cultural and Cross-Media Comparison of Female Nudity in Advertising. *Journal of Promotion Management*, 13 (1), 145–167.

Russo France K., Shah R. H., & Park C. W. (1994). The Impact of Emotional Valence and Intensity on Ad Evaluation and Memory. *Advances in Consumer Research*, 21, 583–588.

DOI: 10.1057/9781137492265.0009

Scrull T. K. (1983). Affect and Memory: The Impact of Affective Reactions in Advertising on the Representation of Product Information in Memory. *Advances in Consumer Research*, 10, 520–525.

DOI: 10.1057/9781137492265.0009

3

Polysemy in Advertising: A Study of the Effects of Advertising Messages on Decision Making

William Chasteen and Shalonda Bradford

▶

Abstract: *This chapter explores the use of polysemy in advertising messages and the varying interpretations consumers have of those messages. In this research we examine television commercials targeted specifically at children to review the differences in how the target audience processes the message as opposed to members of a different age group (e.g., their parents). We further examine the use of imagery and aesthetics in the messages and the effect on consumers' thoughts, feelings, and interpretation of the advertising.*

Keywords: consumer thoughts; effects; messaging; message advertising; polysemy

Arora, Anshu Saxena and Sabine Bacouël-Jentjens. *Advertising Confluence: Transitioning Marketing Communications into Social Movements.* New York: Palgrave Macmillan, 2015. DOI: 10.1057/9781137492265.0010.

DOI: 10.1057/9781137492265.0010

Introduction

Polysemy is defined as the multiple meanings that occur for the same advertising message (Puntoni, Schroeder, & Ritson, 2010). All advertising has a message strategy to get the consumer to feel compelled to buy the product. Researchers continue to develop new ways to appeal to the consumer and have adapted advertising to do that through many forms of technology and communication. The messages that are portrayed for brands can directly affect the longevity and profit for a product. This is why most companies want to adapt messaging to gain a competitive advantage over the competition and earn brand loyalty from the consumer. The techniques used to produce the messages range from radio, print, television, or interactive/Internet ads, and these have been effective and produce a lot of brand loyalty from customers. The only problem with these ads is that times are changing and advertisers have to develop new ways to reach the customers on a global scale. With the global market changing daily advertisers are using new resources like cell phones and the Internet to reach a larger customer base.

Researchers have long studied the effects of advertising messages on consumers (Belch & Belch, 1996; McGuire, 1969; Rothschild, 1987). These studies involve the development of ideas to appeal to certain categories of people and how the people view advertising messages. Companies also study these effects to create the brand image that the company wants. The studies have not been able to show why consumers see different meanings for the same ads. Advertisers design ads with a specific meaning and purpose and sometimes the message is not conveyed to the audience the same way. A fundamental premise of modern marketing thought is that segmentation leads to targeting, which leads to positioning, which then leads to the development of advertising messages (Puntoni, Schroeder, & Ritson, 2010). These messages are designed for a specific market but have the ability to get the intentions of other consumers that the advertisement was not intended for.

This research discusses the imagery used to get the consumers' attention and promote buying behavior. The ideas involve finding specific stimuli that will enhance the advertisement and get the customer thinking about a product. Every consumer will process the stimuli in a different manner and the advertisement can reach a larger spectrum of

DOI: 10.1057/9781137492265.0010

people. Even if the message is intended to be negative, the message may still have a positive effect on some people.

Advertising messages can also be customized by the companies to formulate a brand pattern. For instance, advertisers use sex appeal and gender-specific messages to get the attention of the groups of people. These messages are viewed by some as vulgar and inappropriate, but some marketers are willing to sacrifice public relations to gain exposure and increase profit potential.

Literature review

Marketing literature is dense with discussion of advertising message strategy (e.g., Belch & Belch, 1996; Lee, Nam, & Hwang, 2001; Rothschild, 1987) and various creative typologies (e.g., Bush, Hair, & Bush, 1983; Laskey, Day, & Crask, 1989; Taylor, 1999) of traditional advertising media.

Taylor (1999) defines message strategy as "a guiding approach to a company's or institution's promotional communication efforts for its products, its services, or itself" (p. 7). Quite similar to the dichotomy of informational and transformational messages proposed by Wells (1980) and Laskey, Day, & Crask (1989), Taylor posits that advertising either (1) provides factual information about a product or brand or (2) associates the experience of a product or brand with a set of psychological attributes of consumers. Taylor proposes a comprehensive approach to message strategy using two primary categories of message persuasion subdivided into six segments. The two categories of messages are the informational view and the transformational view. The segments of the informational view include ration, acute need, and routine, whereas ego, social, and sensory are the segments within the transformational view. Advertising using informational messages would impart knowledge about the brand (Taylor, 1999; Wells, 1980). In the ration segment, the advertisement would serve to inform. In the acute need segment, advertising's role would be to increase brand recognition, and in the routine segment, the role of advertising would be to appeal to consumers' rational buying motives (Taylor, 1999). In contrast to the aforementioned category, messages using a transformational strategy would seek to evoke psychological responses about the

DOI: 10.1057/9781137492265.0010

brand that are not commonly associated with the brand (Laskey, Day, & Crask, 1989; Taylor, 1999). In the segment under ego, advertising would appeal to things that are personally important to the consumer, and will "allow the consumer to make a statement to him/herself about who he/she is." In the social segment, advertising appeals are focused on gaining social acceptance or making "a statement to others." The sensory segment uses the five senses to remind consumers of pleasurable experiences (Taylor, 1999). Hwang, McMillan, & Lee's (2003) review of Taylor's model denotes that it was developed using several theoretical frameworks and is grounded in consumers' motivational behaviors. As such, Taylor's model adds value to the current study by providing a streamlined context by which to evaluate polysemy and imagery in advertising messages.

Clow, James, Kranenburg, & Berry (2009) use experimental designs of generic advertising messages to find new strategies to reach a larger market. The model in Figure 3.1 uses techniques that involve illustrative, emotional, and a slice-of-life visual approach (Clow et al., 2009). The ads are the same but the images were changed. The ad was tested using college students involving things that would appeal to them like a backpack and car insurance. Since the results of the testing were hypothetical, the model is a rough idea of what the purchasing behavior for the product would be after seeing the advertisements.

The model shows the measures for attitude toward the written copy and attitude toward the visual were hypothesized to impact both attitude toward the brand and attitude toward the ad (Clow et al., 2009).

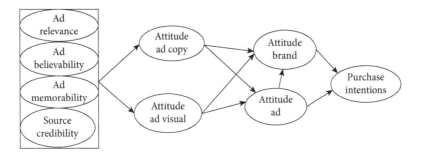

FIGURE 3.1 *Advertisement reaction toward a hypothetical product (Clow et al., 2009)*

DOI: 10.1057/9781137492265.0010

Research reviewing message content supports comprehensive content as having positive effects on consumer behavior (Franke, Huhmann, & Mothersbaugh, 2004). While most research on advertising content tends to focus on attitudinal responses, polysemy is focused on how different people or groups of people get different meanings from the same message (Condit, 1989). Puntoni, Schroeder, & Ritson (2010) define advertising polysemy as "the existence of at least two distinct interpretations for the same advertising message across audiences." In a review of the literature they state, "Despite recent theoretical and managerial developments, no framework has been developed to explain the occurrence of multiple meanings in advertising interpretation. Research into advertising has conventionally focused on the internal content of advertisements, conceptualizing ad comprehension as 'the grasping or extracting of pre-specifiable meanings from the message'" (Mick, 1992: 411). Within this paradigm, the researcher generally decides what the ad "means"—everything else is often labeled as "unintended consequences" (e.g., Pollay, 1986) or "miscomprehension" (e.g., Jacoby & Hoyer, 1982).

The model in Figure 3.2 (Puntoni, Schroeder, & Ritson, 2010) is a framework to discuss the different kinds of polysemy in advertising. The model illustrates how advertisers will use a specific message intended design that is then sent through a medium out to the consumers to become finally decoded into their individual messages. The study shows the four types of polysemy and how the outcomes are all different. The model in Figure 3.2 gives the breakdown of the communication factors involved in the interpretation of advertising messages. The idea projected is to look at alternative perspectives to distinguish between different levels of influence on consumer interpretation processes (Puntoni, Schroeder, & Ritson, 2010). The breakdown goes even further with the nature of the settings the advertisers are using to administer the test and the feelings of the consumer watching the advertisement.

Marketing literature suggests aesthetic attributes influence consumer behavior (Agarwal & Venkatesh, 2002; Chen & Wells, 1999; Stuart, Shim, & Engle, 1997). Often, however, consumers lack the ability to process the content delivered in advertising messages alone (Vakratsas & Ambler, 1999) as is the case with children. The elaboration likelihood (EL) model of persuasion (Petty & Cacioppo, 1986) addresses how persuasive

DOI: 10.1057/9781137492265.0010

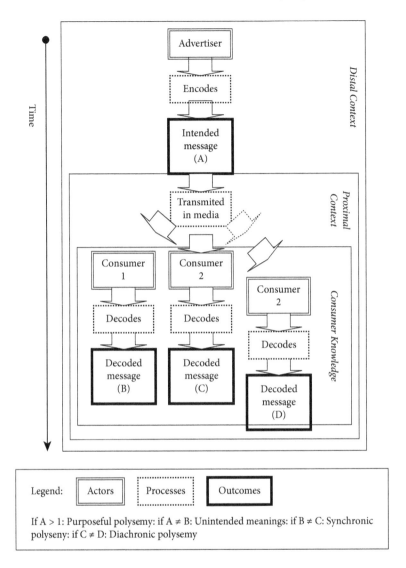

FIGURE 3.2   *Purposeful polysemy (Puntoni, Schroeder, & Ritson, 2010)*

messages influence reactions based on the elaboration (processing) of content. On a continuum of high to low, elaboration (EL) refers to the extent to which the message recipient can think through "issue-relevant" information contained in the message. When EL is high, individuals

DOI: 10.1057/9781137492265.0010

process the information based on the quality of the content. Conversely, when EL is low, persuasion is said to be the result of peripheral cues—such as the quality of the advertisement, perceived attractiveness of the source (Petty & Wegener, 1998) or the presenter (Walker, Feild, Giles, & Bernerth, 2007). The effects of these images seem to be greatest on younger individuals with less personal experience (Behling, Labovitz, & Gainer, 1968; Turban, 2001). These individuals tend to have low EL, and their limited exposure restricts their ability to fully interpret content presented in the advertisements (Walker et al., 2008), thus leaving them more susceptible and easily influenced by messages containing polysemy.

Figure 3.3 (Bakir & Palan, 2010) shows the various factors involved with the children's reactions toward the advertisements. Bakir & Palan's (2010) study highlights the reactions from the children when shown gender-specific advertisements and the attitudes expressed. The last is a timeline of what the ad was about and the designation of the ad to gender. The model proposes children's flexibility toward gender stereotypes is a key variable in determining children's feelings toward both ads and brands (Bakir & Palan, 2010).

Using the accepted models of associative memory found in marketing research (Anderson, 1983; Wyer & Srull, 1989), memory and information of a product brand were conceptualized by Collins & Stevens (2002) as key to the dimensions of brand image. Agrawal & Swaroop's (2009) review of the literature states "brands are important to consumers because (a) brand names offer signals that consumers use to make

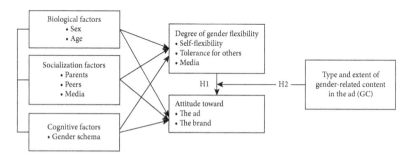

FIGURE 3.3 *Conceptual model for understanding children's attitudes toward ads with gender-related content*

DOI: 10.1057/9781137492265.0010

inference about the attributes of the product, and (b) consumers endeavor to associate themselves with certain brands to improve their self-esteem," and inexperienced consumers are affected more by brand imaging because they tend to use their perceptions to evaluate brands as opposed to making comparisons based on the attributes of the product or service (Aaker, 1991; Keller, 1993). However, the quantity and quality of the information retained is affected by the cognition and perception of the consumer (Benton, Glover, & Bruning, 1983). Psychological literature supports that consumers retain certain information to help them in decision making. McGuire (1969) presents a model that identifies six information-processing phases that affect persuasive communication. They are

(1) presentation of the message
(2) attention to the message
(3) comprehension of its contents
(4) yielding or acceptance of its conclusions
(5) retention of the content
(6) behavior based on their change of mind

Given the numerous variables involved in processing advertising messages, McGuire's six-step process offers a guide to use when examining consumers' information processing of advertising messages. The preceding arguments are conceptualized in a basic model illustrated in Figure 3.4.

Advertising polysemy: conceptual framework

Figure 3.5 illustrates the conceptualized model of advertising polysemy. The model in Figure 3.5 shows the development of messages for advertising and how the consumer interprets those messages.

FIGURE 3.4 *McGuire's advertising interpretation process*

DOI: 10.1057/9781137492265.0010

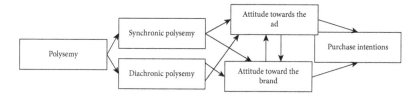

FIGURE 3.5   *Relationship between polysemy and the ad and brand attitudes*

The idea behind Figure 3.5 is to show that advertisers will put out multiple ads and use similar messages for the same idea. After the message is processed and put into a selected format, the consumer has the chance to interpret the message. Not all the messages sent out to the consumers will have the intended interpretation and the customer may not purchase the product being offered. Other consumers will get the intended message and either remember the ad and brand and/or will purchase the product.

Research methodology

We conducted a focus group research where a sample size of 70 undergraduate students at a Historically Black College University (HBCU) was selected for the purpose of the research study, out of which 45 were women. The group was divided into two focus groups of 35 students each. The study was confined to polysemic ads. The category was put together with international ads that might have an impact on a different culture's thoughts and feelings.

First qualitative stage: The ads are presented to the students to see what the difference of opinion is for the male and female psyche. The breakdown would be between the two categories of polysemic ads: synchronic and diachronic. We wanted to introduce the students to both categories and see if there are different feelings provoked based on gender. The result of this stage was a collection of five polysemic ads.

Second qualitative stage: These five stimuli were then presented to 70 undergraduate students of HBCU, in random order for each student. Randomization was used to avoid systematic measurement errors as a result of respondent wear-out. Since the population at a HBCU is

DOI: 10.1057/9781137492265.0010

homogenous with similar socio-demographic characteristics, only gender was included as a classification question. Thereafter, the findings were recorded for these focus groups and generalized for males versus females.

Research findings

After conducting the research, we obtained the results as shown in Appendix I (refer to Tables 3.1–3.4). Women feel more threatened with the sight of blood in the ads. Men have a different thought process when it comes to blood so the affect was not the same. For the sexual ads men tended to be more interested in looking at those ads and focusing on their feelings more.

Brand interest and positive emotion and impression about the brand and an ad lead to positive purchase intention. Polysemy is being categorized with the international ads into two parts (synchronic and diachronic) and the emphasis was on the right feelings being introduced to the correct stimulus.

Conclusion

The research study revisits the concepts of advertising polysemy, and explains how there are certain forms of international polysemy when exposed to different cultures. Men and women have different thoughts and feelings on what an ad should be and how it should make them feel. The idea is to try and pinpoint these factors and get everyone to have the same feeling rather than multiple feelings across the sexes. As of now there is not a formal way to measure polysemy but maybe there is a way to actually control the ad definition to the consumer.

Advertisers have the ability to use any number of variables to try and get a reaction out of a consumer to buy a product or service. The goal is to either set a brand image or to sell a specific product using different methods of visual techniques and word phrases. The advertiser wants to influence the purchase of products through the messages sent through ads that the consumer can visually interpret. These messages can be sent for brand awareness or to make the consumer purchase a product. If the message is clear and interpreted

DOI: 10.1057/9781137492265.0010

in the right manner, the consumer will feel compelled to go make a purchase of the product.

Our research findings are significant with respect to the use of polysemic stimulus. The limitations of the study are that only print ads were used and analyzed, students alone were included, and existing products' ads were used. Future research may focus on the new added dimensions of the two forms of polysemy. Broader sample size will be needed across cultures. Polysemy in advertising appeals must be explored further in the context of brand and ad attitudes and purchase intentions.

Appendix I

TABLE 3.1   *Perceived level of synchronic and diachronic polysemy in ads (1=low, 7=high) for males and females*

Level of	Synchronic	Diachronic	Neutral
Cheerful (Male)	3.5	4.1	3.2
Cheerful (Female)	3.9	3.2	2.9
Insulted (Male)	4.4	3.4	2.8
Insulted (Female)	3.7	3.9	3.8
Irritated (Male)	4.1	4.6	3.8
Irritated (Female)	3.3	3.9	3.5
Interested (Male)	3.8	4.5	2.6
Interested (Female)	4.1	4.0	2.4

DOI: 10.1057/9781137492265.0010

TABLE 3.2   *Summary of exploratory factor analysis results for ad-evoked feelings*

	Cheerful (reverse coded)	Insulted	Irritated	Interested	Carefree (reverse coded)
	Rotated Factor Loadings				
• Pessimistic _____ hopeful	0.777	0.253	0.156	0.284	0.177
• Callous _____ affectionate	0.731	0.265	0.180	0.285	0.172
• Dubious _____ confident	0.662	0.258	0.335	0.229	0.236
• Bad _____ good	0.618	0.462	0.385	0.151	0.024
• Cautious ____ adventurous	0.549	0.353	0.339	−0.018	0.449
• Critical ____ accepting	0.458	0.376	0.394	0.125	0.455
• Insulted _____ honored	0.237	0.754	0.194	0.246	0.153
• Depressed _____ cheerful	0.670	0.282	0.206	0.317	0.293
• Regretful _____ rejoicing	0.368	0.668	0.187	0.219	0.253
• Sad _____ happy	0.423	0.607	0.461	0.100	0.139
• Irritated ____ pleased	0.252	0.224	0.585	0.339	0.224
Worried ___ carefree	0.258	0.326	0.284	0.141	0.784
Nervous ___ calm	0.304	0.260	0.764	0.201	0.269
• Unemotional __ sentimental	0.215	0.174	0.081	0.861	0.266
• Indifferent ____ interested	0.288	0.386	0.266	0.612	0.287
• Contemplative __ impulsive	0.214	0.265	0.287	0.205	0.807
Eigenvalues	3.32	3.27	2.46	1.75	1.60
% of variance	20.77	20.49	15.37	10.92	9.97
Cronbach alpha	0.92	0.84	0.80	0.82	0.82

Extraction method: Principal
Component Analysis
Rotation method: Varimax with
Kaiser Normalization

Rotation converged in seven iterations

KMO and Bartlett's test

Kaiser–Meyer–Olkin measure of sampling adequacy		0.967
Bartlett's test of sphericity	Approx. Chi-Square	19284.226
	Sig.	0.000

DOI: 10.1057/9781137492265.0010

TABLE 3.3 *Correlations between ad-evoked feelings (1=strongest negative feeling; 7=strongest positive feeling)*

Correlations		Worried_carefree	Depressed_cheerful	Insulted_honored	Indifferent_interested	Irritated_pleased	Regretful_rejoicing
Worried_carefree	Pearson correlation	1	0.634**	0.553**	0.498**	0.620**	0.577**
	Sig. (1-tailed)		0.000	0.000	0.000	0.000	0.000
	Covariance	2.835	1.537	1.261	1.222	1.529	1.366
Depressed_cheerful	Pearson correlation	0.634**	1	0.628**	0.536**	0.675**	0.712**
	Sig. (1-tailed)	0.000		0.000	0.000	0.000	0.000
	Covariance	1.537	2.076	1.225	1.125	1.425	1.440
Insulted_honored	Pearson correlation	0.553**	0.628**	1	0.569**	0.620**	0.604**
	Sig. (1-tailed)	0.000	0.000		0.000	0.000	0.000
	Covariance	1.261	1.225	1.835	1.123	1.231	1.150
Indifferent_interested	Pearson correlation	0.498**	0.536**	0.569**	1	0.616**	0.563**
	Sig. (1-tailed)	0.000	0.000	0.000		0.000	0.000
	Covariance	1.222	1.125	1.123	2.125	1.315	1.152
Irritated_pleased	Pearson correlation	0.620**	0.675**	0.620**	0.616**	1	0.636**
	Sig. (1-tailed)	0.000	0.000	0.000	0.000		0.000
	Covariance	1.529	1.425	1.231	1.315	2.146	1.309
Regretful_rejoicing	Pearson correlation	0.577**	0.712**	0.604**	0.563**	0.636**	1
	Sig. (1-tailed)	0.000	0.000	0.000	0.000	0.000	
	Covariance	1.366	1.440	1.150	1.152	1.309	1.973

Note: **Correlation is significant at the 0.01 level (1-tailed).

DOI: 10.1057/9781137492265.0010

TABLE 3.4   *Correlations between types of polysemy*

		Positive Synchronic Polysemy	Negative Synchronic Polysemy	Positive Diachronic Polysemy	Negative Diachronic Polysemy
Positive	Pearson correlation	1	−0.052[*]	0.643[**]	0.032
synchronic	Sig. (1-tailed)		0.018	0.000	0.097
polysemy	Covariance	1.152	−0.056	0.682	0.034
Negative	Pearson correlation	−0.052[*]	1	0.030	0.625[**]
synchronic	Sig. (1-tailed)	0.018		0.115	0.000
polysemy	Covariance	−0.056	1.018	0.030	0.620
Positive	Pearson correlation	0.643[**]	0.030	1	0.110[**]
diachronic	Sig. (1-tailed)	0.000	0.115		0.000
polysemy	Covariance	0.682	0.030	0.976	0.107
Negative	Pearson correlation	0.032	0.625[**]	0.110[**]	1
diachronic	Sig. (1-tailed)	0.097	0.000	0.000	
polysemy	Covariance	0.034	0.620	0.107	0.967

Note: *Correlation is significant at the 0.05 level (1-tailed);
**Correlation is significant at the 0.01 level (1-tailed).

References

Aaker D. A. (1991). *Managing Brand Equity: Capitalizing on the Value of a Brand Name*. New York: Free Press.

Agrawal, R. K., & Swaroop, P. (2009). Effect of Employer Brand Image on Application Intentions of B-School Undergraduates. *The Journal of Business Perspective* , 13 (3), 41–49.

Agarwal R., & Venkatesh V. (2002). Assessing a Firm's Web Presence: A Heuristic Evaluation Procedure for the Measurement of Usability. *Information Systems Research*, 13, 168–186.Anderson J. (1983). *The Architecture of Cognition*. Cambridge, MA: Harvard University Press.

Bakir A., & Palan K. (2010). How Are Children's Attitudes toward Ads and Brands Affected by Gender-Related Content in Advertising? *Journal of Advertising*, 39 (1), 35–48.

Behling O., Labovitz G., & Gainer M. (1968). College Recruiting: A Theoretical Basis. *Personnel Journal*, 47, 13–19.

DOI: 10.1057/9781137492265.0010

Belch G. E., & Belch M. A. (1996). *An Introduction to Advertising and Promotion*. Chicago: Irwin.

Benton S., Glover J. A., & Bruning R. H. (1983). Levels of Processing: Effect of Number of Decisions on Prose Recall. *Journal of Education Psychology*, 3, 382–390.

Brown S. P., & Stayman D. M. (1992). Antecedents and Consequences of Attitude towards the Ad: A Meta-analysis. *Journal of Consumer Research*, 19, 34–51.

Brown M., Bhadury R., & Pope N. (2010). The Impact of Comedic Violence on Viral Advertising Effectiveness. *Journal of Advertising*, 39 (1), 49–65.

Bush A. J., Hair J. F., & Bush R. P. (1983). A Content Analysis of Animation in Television Advertising. *Journal of Advertising*, 12, 20.

Chen Q., & Wells W. D. (1999). Attitude toward the Site. *Journal of Advertising Research*, 5 (1), 27–37.

Clow K., James K., Kranenburg K., & Berry C. (2009). An Examination of the Visual Element Used in Generic Message Advertisements: A Comparison of Goods and Services. *Services Marketing Quarterly*, 30 (1), 69–84.

Collins C., & Stevens C. K. (2002). The Relationship between Early Recruitment-Related Activities and the Application Decisions of New Labor-Market Entrants: A Brand Equity Approach to Recruitment. *Journal of Applied Psychology*, 87 (6), 1121–1133.

Condit, C. M. (1989). The rhetorical limits of polysemy. *Critical Studies in Media Communication*, 6 52), 103–122.

Franke G. R., Huhmann B. A., & Mothersbaugh D. L. (2004). Information Content and Consumer Readership of Print Ads: A Comparison of Search and Experience Products. *Journal of the Academy of Marketing Science*, 32 (1), 20–31.

Hwang J.-S., McMillan S. J., & Lee G. (2003). Corporate Web Sites as Advertising: An Analysis of Function, Audience, and Message Strategy. *Journal of Interactive Advertising*, 3 (2), 10–23.

Keller K. (1993). Conceptualising, Measuring, and Managing Customer-Based Brand Equity. *Journal Marketing*, 57 (1), 1–22.

DOI: 10.1057/9781137492265.0010

Laskey H., Day E., & Crask M. R. (1989). Typology of Main Message Strategies. *Journal of Advertising*, 18 (1), 36–41.

Lee G., Nam K.-T., & Hwang J.-S. (2001). Message Strategy of American and Korean Television Commercial. *Conference of the American Academy of Advertising*. Villanova: Villanova University.

Mackenzie S. B., & Lutz R. J. (1989). An Empirical Examination of the Structural Antecedents of Attitude towards the Ad in an Advertising Pretesting Context. *Journal of Marketing*, 53, 48–65.

McGuire W. (1969, July). An Information Procssing Model of Advertising Effectiveness. *Paper Presented at the Symposium on Behavioral and Management Science in Marketing*. University of Chicago.

Puntoni S., Schroeder J., & Ritson M. (2010). Meaning Matters. *Journal of Advertising*, 39 (2), 51–64.

Petty R., & Cacioppo J. T. (1986). *Communication and Persuasion: Central and Peripheral Routes to Attitude Change*. New York: Springer-Verlag.

Petty R., & Wegener D. T. (1998). Attitude Change Multiple Roles for Persuasion Variables. In D. Gilbert, S. T. Fisk, & G. Lindzey, *The Handbook of Social Psychology*, vol. 2. New York: McGraw Hill, pp. 324–390.

Rothschild M. L. (1987). *Advertising*. Lexington, MA: Heath.

Stuart E., Shim T. A., & Engle R. W. (1987). Classical Conditioning of Consumer Attitudes: Four Experiments in an Advertising Context. *Journal of Consumer Research*, 12, 31–46.

Taylor R. E. (1999). A Six-Segment Message Strategy Wheel. *Journal of Advertising Research*, 39 (6), 7–17.

Turban D. (2001). Organizational Attractiveness as an Employer on College Campuses: An Examination of the Applicant Population. *Journal of Vocational Behavior*, 58, 293–312.

Vakratsas D., & Ambler T. (1999). How Advertising Works: What Do We Really Know? *Journal of Marketing*, 63, 26–43.

Walker J. H., Feild H. S., Giles W. F., & Bernerth J. B. (2008). The Interactive Effects of Job Advertisement Characteristics and Applicant Experience on reactions to Recruitment Messages. *Journal of Occupational and Organizational Psychology*, 81, 619–638.

DOI: 10.1057/9781137492265.0010

Wells W. D. (1980). *How Advertising Works*. Chicago: Needham Harper Worldwide.

Wyer R., & Srull T. K. (1989). Person Memory and Judgement. *Psychological Review*, 96 (1), 58–83.

DOI: 10.1057/9781137492265.0010

4
Does the Country of Origin Matter for Cosmetics? The "Made in France" Argument

Manon Rebufet, Leila Loussaief, and Sabine Bacouël-Jentjens

▶

Abstract: *The market for cosmetics has shown considerable growth in recent years, particularly driven by emerging markets. Many cosmetic brands are present in these countries, competing with French products, which are renowned worldwide. This reputation is mainly based on France's iconic image built through its premium brands. In our research, we question the relevance of the country of origin in the process of consumer decision making and ask representatives of the French cosmetics sector about their assessment. Our overarching research question is: Does the country of origin allow cosmetics to differentiate themselves in the globalized and highly competitive world markets?*

Keywords: consumer decision making; cosmetics; country of origin; France; made in

Arora, Anshu Saxena and Sabine Bacouël-Jentjens. *Advertising Confluence: Transitioning Marketing Communications into Social Movements.* New York: Palgrave Macmillan, 2015. DOI: 10.1057/9781137492265.0011.

Introduction

Globalization, accompanied by the abolition of trade barriers, encouraged the entry of companies into new markets. Consumers are nowadays confronted with a larger supply and multiplied purchasing decision criteria. In this context, after disturbances in 2008 and 2009, the market for cosmetics has returned to the path of growth, particularly driven by emerging markets. Many cosmetic brands are turning up in these countries, competing with French products which are renowned worldwide. The reputation of French cosmetics is mainly based on the iconic image that France wishes to build in particular through its premium brands such as L'Oréal, Louis Vuitton, Hermes, and Chanel.

In this context, it is legitimate to question the relevance of the country of origin in the process of consumer decision making. The objective of this research is to evaluate the importance of this variable in the current context and to analyze the opportunities that professionals have to use this attribute. To address this issue, the article will focus on three parts: The first part presents the concept of the country of origin and its potential impact on the consumer. In the second part, the methodology is discussed. The third part presents the main results of this work.

The concept of country of origin and its impact on consumers

Due to the current economic climate and the maturity of developed markets, companies are looking for new growth opportunities. Foreign markets, such as emerging markets, are a veritable boon for French companies. The international strength of a company comes from the image accrued from the country of origin and the exerted influence on consumers. Indeed, the provenance of a product is a variable that companies put forward when their country has a recognized expertise. However, the realities of the country-of-origin label may be more complex than it seems. In the following, we first put the spotlight on this complexity, before presenting the concept of country image and its impact on the consumer.

DOI: 10.1057/9781137492265.0011

The difficulty of defining the concept of country of origin

Early research on the country of origin dates back to the 1970s. Numerous studies have defined the country of origin as the country of manufacture or assembly of a product (Bilkey & Nes, 1982), this notion was also associated with the "Made in" label (Nagashima, 1977). Nowadays, the conception of a product is scattered over various territories. Raw materials and components often come from countries other than the country of assembly. This context makes the definition of the country of origin more complex. The emergence of new terms as "country of design" or "country of manufacturing" has complicated the understanding of the information for the consumer. The "country of design" refers to the country where the product has been designed and developed. Italy, for instance, is renowned for the quality of its design, especially for certain categories of consumer goods such as shoes. The concept of "Designed in" seems to be preferred by consumers for certain product categories such as luxury goods (Godey, 2009).

The "country of manufacture" is represented by the "Manufactured in" label. Regulations on the country of manufacture are often dubious as they allow indicating the name of a country as long as the last assembly operations have been performed there. Thus the problem of determining the country of origin resides in the fact that companies do not realize all the operations of manufacturing in one unique country. "Country-of-origin" and "country-of-manufacture" labels are more questionable today because of the numerous relocations of major brands (Shirin & Kambiz, 2011). Consumers associate a brand like Louis Vuitton with "Made in France." However, this brand is supplied with components fabricated abroad which are then conditioned and packed in France to get the label "Made in France." Only 45 percent of a product's components must be French to qualify for this appellation. This flexibility concerning the label requirements devalues the impact of the country of origin. Some companies prefer to promote the "Made in Europe" to globalize the provenance of the product and to avoid any potential negative connotation of a specific country. The true role of the "country-of-origin" label is therefore questioned.

"Made in world" is now becoming more common. There is no more one single place reserved for the production of goods, moreover different locations of design and manufacture contribute to their success. In

DOI: 10.1057/9781137492265.0011

fact, companies that decide to produce abroad want to lower costs and hope to respond more quickly and efficiently to local market demands. Products with multiple origins are defined as "hybrid" (Chao, 1993) or "binational" and many studies attempt to explain the importance of the country of origin in this context.

The concept of country image

Similar to brands, countries also possess an image. Indeed, a country image reflects the perceptions—generally stereotypes or subjective representations—assimilated and integrated by consumers about culture, values, and the lifestyles of people in the country. Roth & Romeo (1992) define the notion of the image of the country as the consumer's perception on the country's production and commercial strengths and weaknesses. In a similar vein, other authors relate the country image to its level of industrialization and quality standards (Srikatanyoo & Gnoth, 2002). For Usunier (2006), the country image is built by a combination of stereotypes along with cognitive and affective elements that the consumer manifests with regard to a specific territory.

The concept of "nation branding" implies that the country plays a major role in promoting its expertise, resources, and capabilities internationally. "Nation branding" underlines the history of a country's products and strengthens their attached symbolism (Kapferer, 2011).

In 1997, Nebenzahl and colleagues proposed an analysis of three critical components in the creation of a country image. The first component is cognitive and defines consumers' country perception based on its product categories. The second component is emotional and follows the general opinion about a country through the consumer's subjective emotions and feelings toward this country. The last component is behavioral and describes the consumer's disposition to act vis-à-vis a country.

Today, brands are facing increased competition, more and more demanding consumers, and a constantly changing environment. Originally, brands suggested their nationality through their name and headquarter location. Therefore, the values of a country could be induced. Nowadays, these brands endow additional elements to highlight their nationality. It is therefore important that a country is admired, represents a successful model and a reference. It should also provide consumers with real added value because this creates a veritable link between brands and their consumers and encourages their loyalty. Thus, countries communicate their values by building their communication

DOI: 10.1057/9781137492265.0011

around devices that express their identity. These strategies are implemented in order to strengthen the competitiveness of their local brands internationally and to improve the symbolic representation of the country for consumers (Kapferer, 2011).

The image of the country plays a central role in branding. It helps support the implied warranties of the brand in terms of quality, innovation, and design. But this guarantee is only related to the product if the country shows legitimacy in this sector. For example, it is commonly known that France has expertise in the manufacture of luxury goods (Lou & Davies, 2006). France, as a country, emerges as guarantor of French quality and skills. If France wants to maintain this image attributed by consumers, it must continuously work on the symbols it evokes, and its ability to innovate. This requires that companies and the French population advance the values of the brand mark "France." Emerging economies such as China are trying to improve their image. It is therefore important for these countries to be innovative and develop their own expertise (Ramo, 2007).

The impact of country image on the consumer

First studies on the impact of country of origin on consumers were confined to study only this single variable, which had the effect of falsely increasing the importance of its impact (Usunier, 2006). Latest research shows that when a buyer is faced with a multitude of information with a renowned brand, the importance of the country of origin tends to decrease (Godey et al., 2012). In reality, the impact of the country of origin is moderated by variables such as familiarity with the product or product involvement (Loussaief, 2004).

According to Han (1989; 1990), the influence of the image related to the country of origin can be understood in two ways: the halo effect and the summary construct. The halo effect, also known as cognitive bias, occurs in a context where the consumer is not familiar with a product. The country of origin triggers feelings and a positive or negative perception that the consumer will directly attribute to the product. This influences the perceived product quality, and also consumer beliefs.

The summary construct happens when the consumer knows typical products of a country. Hence, he or she will gather all the information associated with these products in order to transpose to the brands he or she wishes to purchase. The summary construct thus allows a generalization of a certain image to all the brands of a country.

DOI: 10.1057/9781137492265.0011

To make a selection, consumers can rely on extrinsic or intrinsic characteristics of a product. The intrinsic characteristics such as composition, performance, function, or packaging are generally more difficult to assess without a preliminary test of the product. Instead, extrinsic product characteristics such as price, brand, and country of origin are then preferred to assess the quality of the product. A consumer who is not familiar with a product will tend to use extrinsic characteristics. In the case of a purchase, the country-of-origin variable will be more solicited for providing additional quality assurance to the buyer. It is therefore necessary that this information is easy to spot by the client without extensive search.

Other studies have shown that the country image strongly influences the purchasing decisions of consumers (Josiassen & Harzing, 2008), and the perceived quality of products. But this effect varies substantially depending on the category of products studied and the relevance of this variable as selection criteria. Indeed, each country possesses its own expertise and own added value in well-defined areas. France is known for its perfumes, its culinary art, and its luxury brands like Louis Vuitton, Chanel, and Yves Saint Laurent. Consumers therefore base their judgment on the reputation and stereotypes of typical products of the country. In developed countries, goods produced in emerging markets generally do not inspire trust and this information can be a barrier for purchase. For the effect of the country of origin to remain intact, the product should be consistent with the typical production output of that country (Tseng & Balabanis, 2011). The national origin of a product is often expressed by a label, address of the company's headquarter, or the "Made in" written on the packaging of the product. France, for example, is known for its fragrance while Germany stands out for the quality of its cars and machines. It is of importance for these countries to communicate on the origin of their products since the impact on the consumer is considerable (Kotler & Gertner, 2002). It is therefore essential for a French perfume to highlight its origin. The image of France will suggest an expertise for scent, superior perfume ingredients, a prestigious scent composition, and a significant amount of work. The country will therefore support the brand by providing a story, know-how, and symbols that contribute to the positive perception of the product by the consumer.

In the luxury sector, the country of origin may sometimes give way to the brand. Major brand marks such as Guerlain directly suggest French origin of their goods. The name assigned to the brand and to its products

DOI: 10.1057/9781137492265.0011

immediately relates to their country of origin. The Swiss cosmetic brand "La Prairie" or the American cosmetic brand "La Mer" misleads the consumer by suggesting a French origin of their products. It is important to remember that in the universe of cosmetics, the image of the country of manufacture must reflect the image of the brand; otherwise it devalues the perceived image of the product. Brands from countries whose image is positive are more popular with consumers (Norjaya, Mohd, & Osman, 2007). Thus, country of origin still has an important role as decision criteria in high-involvement purchasing processes and can thus become a major argument for consumers.

Methodology

To verify the importance of the country-of-origin variable in practice, a qualitative study was conducted with seven professionals from the hygiene–beauty and more specifically cosmetics sector.

The challenges of the hygiene–beauty market

The market for hygiene and beauty is divided into five broad categories which are skin care, makeup, fragrance, toiletries, and hair care products. This market increased by 27.5 percent since 2007 and was estimated at 433.4 billion dollars in 2012 (Euromonitor, 2013). These results, however, are mixed across countries. In Europe, mainly in Spain, France, Italy, and Greece, the market is stagnant or declining. The sector growth is supported by the good results obtained in the emerging economies. Indeed, in 2012, Asia-Pacific countries generated 48.7 percent of the total for skin care revenues. The European market accounts for 30.8 percent of the total market (total skin care; L'Oréal Finance, 2012). Despite the crisis, the high-end products stay successful as consumers are looking for quality and efficiency.

The market is highly concentrated, with four main actors sharing more than 35.1 percent of the total volume. French actor L'Oréal stands for 11.7 percent of the entire skin care market (Marketline, 2012). Procter & Gamble whose turnover is 20.7 billion USD comes second and Unilever with 18.58 billion USD on third position (WWD, 2012).

France has acquired an international reputation in the field of luxury, fashion, and beauty. However, countries such as Korea, Japan, and

DOI: 10.1057/9781137492265.0011

the United States have gained notoriety by some brand marks such as Erborian, Shiseido, and Clinique.

Cosmetics can be considered luxury items because of their prices and their complex buying process. The category of fragrances, for example, is composed of sophisticated products that reflect a certain social status. The category of care is also expensive and involves health issues. For selection, these products require a careful study of several criteria. Indeed, consumers are interested in the brand, the effectiveness of the products, their ingredients, the price, and the country of origin (Kapferer, 2011).

The interviews

Seven interviews with professionals from the cosmetics sector were conducted as part of this research. The professionals represented primarily French companies operating internationally. All interviews took place in May 2013 either face-to-face or by videoconference. The duration of each interview was between 40 and 90 minutes and followed a standardized interview guide. For reasons of confidentiality, we only refer to the initials of the respondents without mentioning the names of the companies they represent. Table 4.1 describes the profile of each of the participating professionals.

TABLE 4.1   *Profile of interviewed professionals*

Name	Position	Company	Country of activity
CS	International brand director	French cosmetics company positioned in the high-end care segment	France
VV	General manager	US-American company specialized on the makeup segment	China
NP	Commercial manager	French distributor of European cosmetics products for South American markets	Panama
ST	Supervisor travel retail	Group subsidiary handling French brands	Spain
SP	International missions manager	French federation of SME in the cosmetics sector	France
SC	Commercial export manager	French company commercializing shampoo and capillary products	USA
EC	Director Latin America	US branch of French luxury cosmetics brand (skin care, makeup, perfume)	USA

DOI: 10.1057/9781137492265.0011

Findings

Our qualitative study conducted as part of this research reveals three key lessons: the complexity of interpreting the country of origin, the positive and negative potential effects of this variable, and the strategies implemented by companies to exploit the country image.

The country of origin: a complex concept and its impact on the consumer

The country of origin is understood as a complex notion today that can be defined either as the country of manufacture, or the country of design, or the country of invention. For the interviewed professionals, the distinction between the "Made in" and the country of origin exists, but is perceived to be confusing. For some, "The 'Made in' is the place of production while the country of origin may be the place for product design without necessarily producing locally." (ST) "The 'Made in' is the country of manufacture of a product, while the country of origin could be the country of the product's invention or creation." (SC) "The concept of country of origin is somewhat vague, it is the place of manufacturing. The notion of 'Made in' is much clearer. It identifies the place of manufacture and the place of sourcing of the majority of components." (CS)

For professionals, the recurrent use of "Made in" in a globalized world also makes it more difficult for the consumer to understand the information. The misuse of this notion by certain companies deteriorates its impact and creates "confusion in the mind of the consumer" (BV). By some professionals, the "Made in" is perceived as misleading because it can be awarded whenever "a product is assembled in the country 'x' but with imported materials from the countries 'x,' 'y,' and 'z'" (NP). Or the "Made in" is not a label. There is a difference between mandatory labeling and private labels. "Indeed, national labels set up by France to certify the origin and quality of products and 'guaranteed origin' do not fall within the mandatory elements. They are issued and monitored by independent bodies. The 'Made in' then became a concept that has persisted for several years and is nowadays highlighted again" (EC).

Nevertheless, lax regulation concerning the control of the labeling and traceability of ingredients devalue the image of the country of origin.

DOI: 10.1057/9781137492265.0011

"In France, there are regulations on French cosmetics that prohibit the label 'Made in France' if ingredients from a country other than France represent more than 50 percent of the total cost of the product. However, there is no formal control. A company that cheats should (once identified) indicate the country of origin of the majority of their product's components" (CS).

None of the interviewees makes a distinction between invention and manufacture of their products. They are aware that these practices exist for other companies and in other sectors. The jewelry brand Hypanema was particularly cited for its application of the various references to the country of origin. Bracelets are labeled: "Invented in Brazil, Designed in France and Made in China." A special logo has been designed to hide the "Made in China" but to value the exotic appeal of Brazil and the finesse of France. Mentioning France and Brazil allowed the brand to position itself on a high-end segment. These labels are then wrongly used to compensate for the manufacture of the product in a country whose image is negative. These techniques are least approved by the interviewed personnel of cosmetic brands.

The importance of labels depends on the product categories. According to CS, the facial cosmetics labeled "Manufactured in China" but "Designed in France" will still be perceived as of lower quality by the consumer. However, for the makeup segment, the "Designed in" seems to be an alternative to the "Made in." Companies can therefore produce in China without fearing that the product loses its quality image. "Makeup relies not that much on the quality of ingredients but more on the combination of styles, colors and creative ideas" (CS). According to BV, responsible for a makeup brand in China, "the 'Designed in' is an added value, it expresses the creative intention. It helps to justify a premium positioning. This is an additional marketing element." The "Designed in" presents to those companies that cannot produce locally, the advantage to mention countries with a positive connotation. "If our company is growing in the future in the United States, we will opt for the words: 'Made in U.S.' and 'Designed in France'" (SC). According to professionals who market luxury products, the consumers "do not go into detail of the 'Made in,' 'Manufactured in,' 'Designed in' when choosing a cosmetic product. They will probably be guided primarily by the brand image, before checking behind the packaging if there is a 'Made in' to be found" (ST).

DOI: 10.1057/9781137492265.0011

A multitude of references or labels that may be attributed to a product could result in completely neutralizing their effects. Therefore it is important for brands to identify the essential elements to highlight.

The French origin, an advantage for cosmetic brands but sometimes a financial barrier

For a company it is important to identify whether the targeted population discerns the value of the "Made in France" and in which areas it is important to highlight the country of origin. "France enjoys a worldwide reputation, its expertise is recognized by all, whether in the beauty industry or gastronomy, France appears as to be an international surety" (CS).

The recognition of "Made in France" is global. "With the globalization, there are no borders anymore" (EC). The cosmetics professionals recognize France's impact on consumers and international distributors. This argument is regularly integrated into the commercial speech of French cosmetics companies. "The legitimacy of the brand mark 'France' is best known in cosmetics and in particular in the segment of care. [...] is a guarantee of quality in the world without any difference of zones. Its accentuation should not be neglected in any country" (CS).

Nevertheless, the potential importance of the country-of-origin variable in emerging economies should be discussed as well. "The impact of French products is particularly strong in Asia and Russia, where the sensitivity to the country of origin is more powerful" (CS). Indeed, "in emerging markets, consumers need to trust the brand. Counterfeit products are their greatest fear. They fear to consume local products. The country of origin reassures" (BV) or "The impact can be considered superior in emerging countries as we sell dreams" (SC). It is interesting to note that this awareness of "Made in France" is also local. "Today consumers are looking for traceability, they want to become engaged citizens and support economic patriotism. Previously, we offered gifts to clients that were manufactured in China. Currently, over 70 percent of gifts are made in France to strengthen the idea of the protection of the 'Made in France'" (CS).

This raises the issue of relocation. The "Made in France" can then prove to be a barrier to international growth "for the reason that it is more expensive to manufacture in France. French companies are faced

DOI: 10.1057/9781137492265.0011

with high costs of production plus import taxes, which greatly reduce their competitiveness on the international scene" (CS).

For one of the companies surveyed, the country of origin appears to be a barrier to external development. The group operates throughout the world and it continues to produce in France its various product lines. "The 'Made in France' is very important for perfumes and cosmetics. In Brazil we are leaders, it is an important market for us, but taxes are too high. We thought about moving production but we have not done so to keep the 'Made in France.' Asset quality is not the same, neither the quality of packaging. 'Made in France' represents quality and French luxury. The consumer is looking for a unique know-how. More dreams are sold with a brand made in France than made in China" (EC).

Brands want to stay consistent with their history, their DNA, to build confidence among consumers and to encourage brand loyalty. The opinion of the consumer is essential for a luxury brand. Relocation appears to be a bad strategy. "Our group imports its premium brands to China and manufactures locally all product ranges for the local mass market. Chinese consumers would not want to pay more for a product 'made in China'" (CS).

A distinction then emerges between the low-end product brands and luxury brands. It turns out that the luxury brands are mostly part of large groups who have the capacity and financial resources to commercialize a range of products available abroad. SMEs can hardly do the same because of homologation cost, as well as export and import which can be disproportionate in some countries. In addition, the French origin of a product "is an asset for small and medium sized enterprises (SMEs) and its loss would be too risky. For multinationals it is not such a problem since they have big brands" (SP).

The valorization of French origin: Different strategies depending on the brand

In their exploitation of the country of origin, French brands either develop this origin or promote discretion. To study the primordial elements highlighted in internationalization strategies, it is essential to distinguish between SMEs and multinational brand marks. While all companies do not use the "country-of-origin" argument, they nevertheless agree that this variable has an impact on foreign consumers.

The country of origin appears as a central element for luxury cosmetic brands. However, this element is not a directly used argument. "The country of origin is a product attribute. This is common to all French

DOI: 10.1057/9781137492265.0011

cosmetics companies. We will not disclose it because it is not a differentiator" (EC). Koromyslov's (2011) studies on the "Made in France" in luxury confirm that brands like Chanel or Hermes want to keep the label of the French origin of their products but do not communicate directly on this.

At first glance, the country of origin does not seem to be the favored argument. Other product attributes such as packaging or price remain priority. In the case of cosmetics, the brand has a history and it is important not to betray its origins. "Apart from the response to the consumer demand, which is the primary objective of the sale, when we put forward a product it must be consistent with the DNA of the brand. When it comes to makeup or care, we have to highlight the benefits provided by the product which differentiates it from competitors. The country of origin and the quality are naturally arising arguments, because they are part of the brand's DNA" (ST).

In the field of fragrances, the brand name occurs first as it often evokes the creator's name. "It is not the new product launches that build the brand; but the brand should guide the attributes of new launches. Common values in each Givenchy product are for instance: aristocratic elegance, magnetic beauty, spontaneous style and luxury. Based on this one can easily recognize more or less successful launches [...] the consumer must be able to identify with the product attributes if you want it to be a success" (ST).

For French SMEs, a toponymic name is not enough to challenge the consumer. Many foreign companies use the French semantics to influence buyers, diminishing consequently the impact of the brand name on purchasing decisions. For a skincare brand, the national origin comes after the benefits of the product. Indeed, "it is necessary that the brand can convince that it responds to the specifics of the local market. As an example, L'Oréal's products are based on Western culture but marketed by local beauty icons." The country of origin will be highlighted in these communications by symbols, labels, commercial speech, and any communication strategy underlining the French provenance.

It is however difficult to generalize this view for all French brands. For multinationals, the country of origin cannot be used as such an argument, but is usually suggested by some elements such as the city often displayed under the brand name. By contrast, SMEs may use logos that contain graphical elements to evoke a country of origin, for instance a stylized Eiffel Tower.

DOI: 10.1057/9781137492265.0011

Conclusion

The notion of country of origin regained in importance in recent years and its significance is growing again in France since 2011. Globalization has contributed to the development of international trade and encouraged firms to produce in countries with low costs.

Our research has analyzed the impact of the country of origin on consumers of French cosmetics abroad from a point of view of mostly French cosmetics professionals. The findings show that the country of origin has a growing importance in the context of market globalization. Countries work on their image in order to enhance the value of their companies internationally. Indeed, the "Made in France" is still a sales argument for multinationals and SMEs. For some companies, France remains undoubtedly the country of luxury and beauty.

Although the argument of the country of origin is not always comprehended by consumers, it affects in a sustainable manner the image of the brand and its products. The country of origin is part of the brand's capital, proving products with a veritable added value. In cosmetics, consumers are looking for guarantee for and respect of the values of the brand. Companies then adapt to some extent their strategies to make best use of this element.

The incidence of the country-of-origin variable is likely to evolve over the coming years. It will be interesting to analyze to what extent these changes will be made. The country of origin currently allows French cosmetics companies to assert their legitimacy and excellence, but what will happen when foreign competitors will respond and try to enter these markets? These challenging issues make our research more meaningful in the global context.

References

Bilkey W. J., & Nes E. (1982). Country-of-Origin Effects on Product Evaluation. *Journal of International Business Studies*, 13, 89–99.

Chao P. (1993). Partitioning Country of Origin Effects: Consumer Evaluations of a Hybrid Product. *Journal of International Business Studies*, 24 (2), 291–306.

Euromonitor. Beauty and Personal Care, <http://www.portal.euromonitor.com/Portal/Pages/Magazine/IndustryPage.aspx>, May 11, 2013.

DOI: 10.1057/9781137492265.0011

Godey, B., Pederzoli, A., Aiello, G. & Donvito, R. et al. (2012). Brand and Country-of-Origin Effect on Consumers' Decision to Purchase Luxury Products. *Journal of Business Research*, 65 (10), 1461–1470.

Han M. C. (1989). Country Image: Halo or Summary Construct. *Journal of Marketing Research*, 25, 222–229.

Han M. C. (1990). Testing the Role of Country Image in Consumer Choice Behaviour. *European Journal of Marketing*, 24–40.

Josiassen A., & Harzing A. W. (2008). Descending from the Ivory Tower: Reflections on the Relevance and Future of Country-of-Origin Research. *European Management Review*, 5 (4), 264–270.

Kapferer J. N. (2011). France: Pourquoi penser marque? Revue française de gestion – N° 218–219, 13–23.

Koromyslov M. (2011). Le « Made in France » en question. Revue française de gestion – N° 218–219, 107–122.

Kotler P., & Gertner D. (2002). Country as Brand, Product, and Beyond: A Place Marketing and Brand Marketing Perspective. *Journal of Brand Management*, 9, 249–261.

L'Oréal Finance (2012). L'Oréal Rapport d'activité 2012, <http://www.loreal-finance.com/_docs/pdf/rapportannuel/2012/LOREAL_Rapport-Activite-2012_FR.pdf>; accessed August 12, 14.

Lou T., & Davies G. (2006). Branding China: The Ultimate Challenge in Reputation Management. *Corporate Reputation Review*, 9 (3), 198–210.

Loussaief L. (2004). La sensibilité du consommateur à l'origine nationale perçue des marques: une variable modératrice de l'effet de l'image d'un pays sur la qualité perçue d'un produit, 20ème Congrès de l'AFM - Saint-Malo.

Marketline. Industry Profile Global Skincare November 2012. http://www.marketline.com/sectors-and-roles/marketing/> accessed May 10, 2013.

Nagashima A. (1977). A Comparative 'Made-in' Product Image Survey among Japanese Businessmen. *Journal of Marketing*, 41, 95–100.

Nebenzahl I. D., Jaffe E. D., & Lampert S. I. (1997). Towards a Theory of Country Image Effect on Product Evaluation. *Management International Review*, 37, 27–49.

Norjaya M. Y., Mohd N. N., & Osman M. (2007). Does Image of Country-of-Origin Matter to Brand Equity?. *Journal of Product & Brand Management*, 16 (1), 38–48.

Ramo J. C. (2007). *Brand China*. London: Foreign Policy Centre.

DOI: 10.1057/9781137492265.0011

Roth, M. S. & Romeo, J. B. (1992). Matching Product Category and Country Image Perceptions: A Framework for Managing Country-of-Origin Effects. *Journal of International Business Studies*, 23 (3), 477–497.

Shirin K., & Kambiz H. (2011). The Effect of the Country-of-Origin Image, Product Knowledge and Product Involvement on Consumer Purchase Decisions. *Chinese Business Review*, 10 (8), 601–615.

Srikatanyoo N., & Gnoth J. (2002). Country Image and International Tertiary Education. *Journal of Brand Management*, 10 (2), 139–148.

Tseng H. T., & Balabanis G. (2011). Explaining the Product-Specificity of Country-of-Origin Effects. *International Marketing Review*, 28 (6), 581–600.

Usunier J. C. (2006). Relevance in Business Research: The Case of Country-of-Origin Research in Marketing. *European Management Review*, 3, 60–73.

WWD. WWD Beauty Inc's Top 100: The Top 10. <http://www.wwd.com/beauty-industrynews/financial/wwd-beauty-incs-top-100-the-top-10–6142686> accessed May 13, 2013.

DOI: 10.1057/9781137492265.0011

5

Brand Diffusions and Brand Naming Strategies

Eric Billinger and Amit Arora

Abstract: *The research study examines a company's ability to create brand equity within its sub-brand when employing diffusion branding. Brand equity is the importance of a brand within the minds of consumers based on their experiences with the brand over time. Diffusion brands are step-down line extensions of existing luxury brands, normally less expensive than the mainline products. This study explores three types of brand naming strategies in addition to the well-known brand extension strategsy for building brand equity and investigates customers' perceptions of brand image when using brand naming strategies. Such findings can be useful to help reduce failures when implementing brand diffusions and extension programs and thus improve overall consumer response to diffused brands.*

Keywords: brand equity; brand extension; brand image; brand loyalty; brand naming; diffusion brands; parent brands

Arora, Anshu Saxena and Sabine Bacouël-Jentjens. *Advertising Confluence: Transitioning Marketing Communications into Social Movements.* New York: Palgrave Macmillan, 2015. DOI: 10.1057/9781137492265.0012.

Introduction

This year shoppers are feeling less shy about spending money, and department stores are happily stocking up with appealing—and often luxury—merchandise for the holiday season. This positive attitude toward spending might be surprising because in the past several years we have experienced many negative events, including terrorist attacks in America, a global outbreak of SARS, the war in Iraq, and a financial crisis which resulted in the global luxury market shrinking. Nevertheless, luxury brands like Moët Hennessy Louis Vuitton (LVMH), the world's biggest luxury goods company by sales, Burberry, a British clothing firm, and PPR, a French retail and luxury group, are reporting double digit sales growth (The Economist, 2010).

The demand for luxury products is motivated by the underlying factor of status through the display of wealth (Eastman, Goldsmith, & Flynn, 1999). Established the concept of status consumption, where people often consume luxury products to exhibit status to self and to others. Diffusion branding occurs when a company creates a second product line which appeals to a different target market than the target market of the parent company. By launching a diffusion brand, a parent luxury brand enters an entirely new market of luxury, also referred to as affordable luxury. A diffusion brand is identified as a step-down brand extension of an existing luxury brand in similar product categories, which aims to establish a close connection with the parent brand as a luxury product (Fernie, Moore, Lawrie, & Hallsworth, 1997). Diffusion brands allow the younger population to experience the possession of luxury items at an affordable price to display wealth.

Brand equity has become essential for many organizations because it creates several marketing advantages and increases companies' customer loyalty. Examples of popular fashion diffusion brands with high brand equity include Armani—Armani Exchange, Fendi—Fedisimme, and Calvin Klein—CK Jeans. These luxury companies attract wealthy customers which sustains a high status image for other customers. Wearing luxury clothes symbolizes success which individuals wish to exemplify.

The success of diffusion brands is often determined by a **brand naming strategy**. If a diffusion brand like Armani Exchange has the name of the *parent* brand incorporated into its name the benefits reaped from Armani's existing status are almost immediate. However, if a new brand

DOI: 10.1057/9781137492265.0012

is given a completely new name like Miu Miu of Prada, the benefits are much less apparent. To expand the understanding of brand naming, this research examines an organization's ability to create brand equity within their sub-, nested, and new brands when employing diffusion branding. This chapter investigates the following questions:

▸ How do consumers view diffusion brands?
▸ What are the positive and negative effects of diffusion brands?
▸ Do diffusion brands have similar levels of brand equity as their parent brands?

Yoo et al. (2000) notes that by introducing key aspects of brand equity one can create brand-building activities or brand-harming activities. For example, creating too many sub-brands may result in a dilution of the equity of the parent brand.

In addition, a downside is that any negative traits connected with the parent brand are associated with the new brand. A new brand name must create an image and personality for itself. For example, Virgin's brands are an odd collection of sub-brands, such as trans-Atlantic flights, records, cola, lingerie, electricity, trains, concerts, and mobile phones. Many of Virgin sub-brands seem poorly thought out and are not a leading brand in any of its businesses. Whether it is flights, electricity, or music, Virgin is simply one of the market players (The Economist US, 2010).

This chapter presents the theoretical background by reviewing the literature on diffusion brands, brand equity, brand naming, and parent brands. This background leads to the formulation of relevant hypotheses. Next, the research methodology and the analysis of the results are presented. The chapter concludes with discussion of findings and managerial implications.

Literature review

Brand extension

The term "Brand Extension" refers to new launches that use an established brand to enter new product categories (Aaker & Keller, 1990). There are three types of extensions including range, line, and brand extensions. They are techniques to position brand extension either closer to or further away from the parent brand. A model has been adapted

DOI: 10.1057/9781137492265.0012

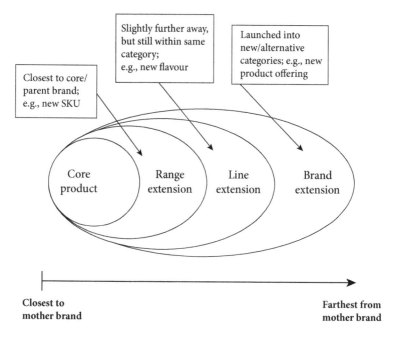

FIGURE 5.1   *Forms of extensions*

from Taylor (2004) to define and depict these three types of extensions in Figure 5.1. The model divides the product extension that creates a brand into four categories, which include core product, range extension, line extension, and brand extension; then those four categories are assembled along two categories that measure their distance from the parent brand.

Diffusion brand

A diffusion brand is a type of brand extension, whereby a new product is introduced under the name of an existing brand (Aaker, 1991). Also known as "second lines," they are step-down line extensions of existing luxury brands, normally less expensive than the mainline merchandise (Beaudoin, Lachance, & Robitaille, 2003). A positive view of a diffuse brand can only be achieved when customers perceive that the sub-brand has inherent qualities of the parent brand. Aaker & Keller (1990) posited that a positive attitude toward a brand extension was influenced by the three main-effect brand extension "fit"

DOI: 10.1057/9781137492265.0012

attributes—namely complementarity, substitutability, and transferability—and the indirect effect of original brand quality moderated by the "fit" attributes.

Perceived fit is a determinant for the success of a brand extension. The perception of fit allows consumers to establish common ground between the parent brand and its diffusion brand. This commonality helps to determine a desired positioning relative to the parent brand to achieve similar product quality and brand image assessment (Bridges, Keller, & Sood, 2000). It is essential that the extension's image is similar to that of the parent brand so consumers are more likely to view the extension as a typical member of the parent product category to achieve more positive evaluation. Category-based processing predicts that similar extensions, for example, Tropicana orange juice, should be rated higher than dissimilar extensions like Tropicana cola. The parent brand knowledge retrieved is more relevant in similar extension categories (Aaker & Keller, 1990). To measure the consumer assessment of diffusion brands, the literature suggests the use of product quality, brand image, and purchase intention as indicators. Product quality, for example, assesses whether the product delivers the benefits that consumers truly desire for need satisfaction (Keller, 1998). The desired positioning of a diffusion brand can be achieved via different brand naming strategies.

Brand naming

When companies decide they want to create a new product to enter a new market, they must decide the name for this new product and the launching strategy. Desai & Keller (2002) show that the type of **brand naming strategy** significantly influences the acceptance of extensions. The four different brand naming approaches companies use to name new products are brand extension, new brand, sub-branding, and nested branding. Brand extension uses the existing brand name on the new product (e.g., Snickers Ice Cream Bars). A new brand is when a parent company creates an entirely different name for the subsequent product (e.g., Coca-Cola has Fruitopia). Sub-branding is when a company uses its recognizable name adjacent to the new brand such as the brands discussed earlier (Armani Exchange from Armani and CK from Calvin Klein). Nested brands occur when a company introduces a new brand or line (e.g., Dockers by Levi's).

DOI: 10.1057/9781137492265.0012

Brand equity

Brand equity is sometimes defined imprecisely. Aaker (1991) provided a more comprehensive definition of brand equity as "A set of brand assets and liabilities linked to a brand, its name and symbol that add or subtract from the value provided to a firm and/or to that firm's customers." Companies can create brand equity for their products by making them memorable, easily recognizable, and superior in quality and reliability. Brand equity can be thought of as the "added value" endowed to a product in the thoughts, words, and actions of consumers (Yoo, Donthu, & Lee, 2000). Mass marketing campaigns can also help to create brand equity.

Brand image

Brand image is the perception about a brand that is reflected by the brand association held in the consumers' memory (Aaker, 1991). It is the current view of the customers about a brand and it signifies what the brand presently stands for. Brand image is the overall impression in consumers' minds that is formed from all sources. As consumers are exposed to a brand's advertising more frequently, they develop not only higher brand awareness and associations, but also a more positive perception of brand quality, which leads to strong brand image and loyalty. Brand image is developed over time through advertising campaigns with a consistent theme and is authenticated through the consumers' direct experience.

Conceptual framework

In this research, we try to investigate the effectiveness of diffusion branding and customers' perception of quality when using different types of brand naming strategies.

The model in Figure 5.2 represents the elements required in creating a diffusion brand leading to either a positive or negative customer perception. A positive customer perception of the parent brand and the brand extension leads to a positive customer response in purchasing the second line product. A connection must be made in the consumer's mind that the parent brand has reliability in the second line's field to

DOI: 10.1057/9781137492265.0012

FIGURE 5.2   *Creation of diffusion brands*

lead to a positive attitude toward the extension. A negative customer perception of the parent brand is made when the new product does not have favorable brand equity, image, loyalty, and awareness. This negative perception can lead to a failed product launch.

The brand extension naming strategy can lead to positive customer perception of the diffused product if consumers can see a perfect fit between the new product and the parent brand. Managers should use this strategy if the parent brand has consistency in the field that the product is being marketing in. This strategy should not be used if the company is attempting to penetrate a completely new market. Consumers will not see the fit between the brand and the product which will lead to negative customer perception of the diffused product.

The conceptual framework of the study is shown in Figure 5.2 to illustrate relationships between various brand-related elements. Hem, Chernatony, & Iverson (2001) suggest that all companies can benefit from adopting a master brand strategy, where the company name becomes the "umbrella" over all products and services. Keller (2003) contended that brand equity must start from the perspectives of consumers. From that perspective, brand equity means the differences in brand knowledge among consumers about the marketing stimulus effect given by a certain brand.

DOI: 10.1057/9781137492265.0012

Based on the conceptual framework, we formulate the following hypothesis:

> H1: Young status-oriented consumers who are *brand loyal* will positively evaluate diffusion brands regardless of the different brand naming strategies.

Research methodology

The hypothesis was assessed by using the parent and hypothetical diffusion brands of a real luxury (fashion) brand generated through three naming strategies. The chosen brand was "Armani" with the fictitious name of "Aspiration" which was inserted into the parent brand to formulate

- a sub-brand (Armani Aspiration),
- a nested brand (Aspiration by Armani), and
- a new brand (Aspiration).

Data were collected from 371 students (18–28 years old) in a US university, out of whom 209 young adults were found to be status conscious and brand loyal. The scales are given in Tables 5.1 and 5.2. Two hundred and nine student samples were further used for quantitative analyses; of these students 83.7 percent (175) were females. Scale reliabilities (Cronbach alpha) for status consumption and brand loyalty were between 0.7374 and 0.7808, which are deemed acceptable by Nunnally (1978). Much of the brand extension research has made use of student samples to evaluate extension products (e.g., Aaker & Keller, 1990; Bhat & Reddy, 2001; Van Osselaer & Alba, 2003). DelVecchio (2000) and Yavas (1994) proposed that a student sample can be representative of general consumers.

Results

The ANOVA tests revealed no significant difference in brand image evaluation between the parent brand and its diffusion brands. There is partial support for our hypothesis, and we found that

- There is no difference in brand image evaluation between the parent brand and its sub-brand.
- However, there is significant difference in brand image evaluation between the parent brand and its nested as well as new brand (as shown in Table 5.3).

DOI: 10.1057/9781137492265.0012

TABLE 5.1   *Brand loyalty scale (adapted from Lau & Lee, 1999)*

1. I intend to keep buying *(the brand)*.
2. If another brand is having a sale, I will generally buy the other brand instead of *(the brand)*.
3. If *(the brand)* is not available in the store when I need it, I will buy it another time.
4. If *(the brand)* is not available in the store when I need it, I will buy it somewhere else.
5. If someone makes a negative comment about *(the brand)*, I would defend it.
6. I would recommend *(the brand)* to someone who cannot decide which brand to buy in this product class.
7. I would believe a person if that person made a negative comment about *(the brand)*.
8. I often tell my friends how good *(the brand)* is.

TABLE 5.2   *Status consumption scale (adapted from Eastman, Goldsmith, & Flynn, 1999)*

1. I am interested in new products with status.
2. I would buy a product just because it has status.
3. I would pay more for a product if it has status.
4. The status of a product is irrelevant to me.
5. A product is more valuable to me if it has some snob appeal.

TABLE 5.3   *Diffusion brands vis-à-vis brand image of product*

	Brand Image		
	Mean	*t*-Value	Sig.
Parent brand			
Armani	5.28	0.35	0.142
Sub-brand			
Armani Aspiration	4.81	−1.3	0.465
Nested brand			
Aspiration by Armani	5.65	2.46	0.045*
New brand			
Aspiration	5.69	2.52	0.049*

Note: *Significant at 0.05 level.

DOI: 10.1057/9781137492265.0012

In order to discuss our results further, we now present three case studies for diffusion branding.

Case studies on diffusion branding

Case study 1: Courtyard by Marriott

Courtyard by Marriott opened its first hotel in 1983. Since its conception, the hotel chain has opened over 900 hotels in 35 countries. Courtyard was introduced by the parent brand, Marriott, and is a nested brand. Strategically this is the best choice as a brand naming strategy. Marriott has a high middle class to low high class standard of hotels and Courtyard fits directly into this group. However, Courtyard has different and distinct features that separate it from the original Marriott hotel brand; therefore, it can be independently called "Courtyard." Marriot has six different hotels that fit into the upper middle/low high class hotel category, and they are all nested brands. This naming strategy tells the consumer that at each hotel chain they will receive standard Marriott quality but a different hotel experience. For example, Courtyard's buildings are built low to seem less commercial and more welcoming with a built-in restaurant while Fairfield Inn by Marriott is more concerned with having economical prices with limited services beyond the room.

Courtyard by Marriott's uniformity ensures that customers know what they are getting when they walk into one of their hotels. This consistency of experience ensures that happy customers will become (and stay) brand loyal. It also creates a good image for Marriott as a whole. If travelers want to stay at a Courtyard, but it is not in the city they are visiting, they very well may stay in another Marriott nested brand because of their satisfactory, past experience with Courtyard.

Marriott has chosen the proper brand naming strategy for Courtyard and other hotels in that market segment. Marriott's successful brand naming strategy has allowed Courtyard to thrive in the past 30 years, and its successes have enabled the company to grow.

Case study 2: Xerox

Xerox's brand name is so strong that it has become a verb in everyday speech. In 1959 the Xerox 914 was launched as the first automatic plain

DOI: 10.1057/9781137492265.0012

paper copier; it could make seven copies in a minute. The product was a huge success and attracted plenty of media attention. It quickly became a must-have product for any business. In 1961 the Xerox Corporation was listed on the New York Stock Exchange, and in less than ten years after that first copier, sales for Xerox reached the $1 billion mark (US).

Xerox had tried two types of brand naming strategies, sub-branding and brand extension. The company's first computer named Xerox Data system was released 15 years after its first automatic copier. By this time, the company had such a stranglehold on the copying category of office supplies that consumers could not see Xerox as a company that produced anything well other than copiers. The company name became a synonym for copy, and even if companies had a Canon or Kodak copier employees would still say, "Xerox these for me." Xerox' sub-brand, XTEN network, was also unsuccessful. The failed product ventures illustrate that a strong brand name is not enough to have a successful product. Xerox was cursed with having a successful one-product monopoly.

With both of these products, Xerox should have used the new product naming strategy. Xerox had such a strong brand name in copiers it should have done everything possible to separate the new products from the parent brand. Without hearing the name Xerox, consumers would have been able to judge the products based on their attributes alone and separate from the idea that Xerox could only be good at making copiers. The company's research facility turned out a lot of useful and innovative products; if the Xerox name had not been so closely attached to the final products that left the facility, the company may have been more successful in other office product categories, given, of course, that effective marketing and advertising strategies were in place to introduce the new names to the market.

Case study 3: Armani exchange

Giorgio Armani is an Italian luxury company founded in 1975. It has had many successful diffused brands including AX (Armani Exchange), AJ (Armani Jeans), Armani Collezioni, and Emporio Armani. AX was launched in the United States in 1991 in order to reach a large target market. The clothing was more affordable than its prestigious counterparts Collezioni and Emporio. AX has over 200 stores globally and has been a successful sub-brand from Armani. AX sells casual street clothes and accessories while the other outlets produce high-end suits.

DOI: 10.1057/9781137492265.0012

Creating a sub-brand to sell chic street clothes was a good decision by Armani. Consumers that shop at AX know that they will be getting Armani quality, at more economical prices, in the nonformal clothing category. Consumers are not thinking that they are wearing "cheap" luxury clothes; rather, they are wearing an Armani design from Italy. This perception is because of the strategic brand name Armani Exchange. Exchange is not separated enough from Armani that it can survive on its own like Courtyard; it needs the successful name of Armani to piggy-back on in order to be appealing to customers, which it has done. The consumer is able to see a good (and strong) fit between the parent brand Armani and its sub-brand AX, and this has led to a successful clothing venture.

Managerial implications

This research introduced the brand naming strategies—sub-brand, nested brand, and new brand—to show that the product name has significant implications in the success or the failure of the product. A great deal of research goes into what new products will be named and how they will be introduced to the consumer. We have seen competitive products, like the Xerox Data Processor, fail because of the company's naming strategies and consumers' judgmental attitude toward them. A company must hypothesize what the consumer's attitude toward the product will be when using different brand diffusion naming strategies. Companies should take samples of different names for their products and record consumers' attitudes toward each name. This analysis will allow them to select the name which gives the product the best chance for success. A name which elicits a positive fit and attitude in the mind of the consumer should be chosen.

The research provided here has been applied to the western and European world; however, there are different strategies used in Asia. Companies like Yamaha, Mitsubishi, and Hyundai (from Japan and South Korea) were able to succeed in their economies selling products across different categories. Yamaha produces guitars, motorcycles, pianos, archery equipment, and much more. Mitsubishi sells vehicles, speakers, and batteries. In Asia, many products are able to be success-ful without having a clear product fit with the parent company. More research is needed on this topic.

DOI: 10.1057/9781137492265.0012

Conclusion

The goal of this chapter is to present a conceptual framework that would provide a useful structure for companies developing brand strategies and researchers studying brand extensions. Particularly, the chapter builds a theoretical foundation based on past research in consumer perception that should be helpful in addressing some of the new challenges in developing brand strategies that have arisen because of changes in the marketing environment. While many of the ideas expressed in this research may be familiar to companies, its value is in integrating these various notions to provide a more comprehensive picture of how marketers can create value for a brand through diffusions.

The research has managerial implications for advertisers who should market nested and new brands more rigorously in order to keep reminding the customer about their connection with the parent brand. Differential advertising strategies along with differential budgets can help companies maintain and/or build their client base as they are advertising sub-, nested, and/or new brands.

References

Aaker D. A. (1991). *Managing Brand Equity*. New York: Free Press.

Aaker D. A., & Kevin Lane Keller (1990). Consumer Evaluations of Brand Extensions. *Journal of Marketing*, 54, 27–41.

Beaudoin P., Lachance M. J., & Robitaille J. (2003). Fashion Innovativeness, Fashion Diffusion and Brand Sensitivity among Adolescents. *Journal of Fashion Marketing and Management*, 7(1), 23–30.

Bridges S., Keller D. L., & Sood S. (2000). Communication Strategies for Brand Extensions: Enhancing Perceived Fit by Establishing Explanatory Links. *Journal of Advertising*, 29(4), 1–11.

Cheong E., & Phau I. (2003). *Young Status Oriented Consumers' Evaluation of Diffusion Brand Extensions: The Effects of Brand Loyalty*, ANZMAC Adelaide.

Desai K. K., & Keller K. L. (2002). The Effects of Brand Expansions and Ingredient Branding Strategies on Host Brand Extendibility. *Journal of Marketing*, 66, 73–93.

DOI: 10.1057/9781137492265.0012

Eastman J. K., Goldsmith R. E., & Flynn L. R. (1999). Status Consumption in Consumer Behavior: Scale Development and Validation. *Journal of Marketing Theory and Practice*, vol. Summer, 41–52.

Fernie J., Moore C., Lawrie A., & Hallsworth A. (1997). The Internationalization of the High Fashion Brand: The Case of Central London. *Journal of Product and Brand Management* 6(3), 151–162.

Hem L. E., Chernatony L., & Iverson N. M. (2001). Factors Influencing Successful Brand Extension. Norwegian School of Economics and Business Administration, pp. 4–37.

Keller K. L. (1998). *Strategic Brand Management: Building, Measuring, and Managing Brand Equity*. Upper Saddle River, NJ: Prentice Hall.

Keller K. L. (2003). *Strategic Brand Management: Building, Measuring, and Managing Brand Equity*, 2d Edn. Upper Saddle River, NJ: Prentice Hall.

Lau, G. T., & Lee, S. H. (1999). Consumers' trust in a brand and the link to brand loyalty. Journal of *Market-Focused Management*, 4 (4), 341–370.

Mason R. S. (1981). *Conspicuous Consumption: A Study of Exceptional Consumer Behaviour*. Farnborough: Gower Publishing Company Limited.

Taylor D. (2004). *Brand Stretch: Why 1 and 2 Extensions Fail, and How to Beat the Odds*. Chichester: John Wiley & Sons Ltd.

The Economist US (2010). Bling Is Back; Luxury Goods. (A Surprising Recovery in Luxury Goods). Economist Newspaper Ltd. HighBeam Research. http://www.highbeam.com/doc/1G1-240031712.html.

Yoo B., Donthu N., & Lee S. (2000). An Examination of Selected Marketing Mix Elements and Brand Equity. *Journal of the Academy of Marketing Science*, 28(2), 195–211.

DOI: 10.1057/9781137492265.0012

6

Say It without Saying It: How Consumers Interpret "Tropes" in Advertising and Its Impact on Campaign Success

Jamin Gordon and Jun Wu

▶

Abstract: *As consumers we are subject to various mediums of advertising including print, radio, and commercials. The going trend in advertising is to have a witty trope or metaphor which appeals to consumers. Each consumer interprets these tropes differently, creating a difference in opinions toward the advertised product. The success of an advertising campaign weighs heavily on how consumers will receive a particular message. This research introduces the RURRAL framework, a new innovative framework which determines if an advertising campaign is successful.*

Keywords: ad and brand attitudes; advertising recall; figurative language; metaphors; RURRAL framework; tropes

Arora, Anshu Saxena and Sabine Bacouël-Jentjens. *Advertising Confluence: Transitioning Marketing Communications into Social Movements.* New York: Palgrave Macmillan, 2015. DOI: 10.1057/9781137492265.0013.

Introduction

According to Merriam-Webster Learner's Dictionary, the word trope is defined as a word, phrase, or image used in a new and different way in order to create an artistic effect. Another definition for trope is a word or expression used in a figurative sense. These two definitions when partnered together create the crux of many advertisements. Tropes are expressed through figurative language, pictures, and digital effects in commercials. Tropes can be highly effective in conveying a message if they are presented in the correct context to the correct audience. It is imperative to remember that although a particular trope or metaphor presented in an advertisement may prove to be positively appealing to one audience it may create raves for a dissimilar audience. Various phrases, gestures, as well as colors differ in meaning throughout the world. For instance, in America it is rude to slurp; conversely it is considered good table manners in Japan. The same rule applies when creating advertisements for various cultures, subcultures, and age groups. In addition it is proven that tropes influence persuasiveness as well as memorability in advertisements (Toncar & Munch, 2003). In order for an advertisement to be effective, you must know the likes and dislikes as well as what is appropriate or not appropriate for your target market.

The comprehension of a trope in an advertisement can elevate a campaign to prodigious success but if the consumer is left feeling perplexed the campaign may result in epic failure. Consumers may interpret tropes in various ways. Depending on what is displayed or written in the trope, consumers may interpret it in a sexual, emotional, sarcastic, literal, or humorous context. In some cases the consumer may not understand the trope and thereby is unable to produce an interpretation. These interpretations are not always mutually exclusive. Trope advertising may trigger several interpretations at once or altered interpretations upon each viewing. Although the consumer is decoding the trope, the message received may not be the intended message of the company.

Examples of commercials using tropes include the York Peppermint Patty Pieces commercial ending in the tagline "All Your Favorites in Pieces," Trojan Condoms using the tagline "You Can't Wait to get it on," Smirnoff with the closing voice-over "It's Like Having a Bartender in Your Cooler," as well as Old Spice's Scent Vacation with the tagline "Become one of the Freshest Smelling Places on Earth." Tropes are also

DOI: 10.1057/9781137492265.0013

presented in print ads. Some print ads with tropes include Absolut Blank "It All Starts with an Absolut Blank," Dolce Gusto "It's Great to Change Every Day; Coffee is not Just Black," and Got Milk?, "I'm Sorry I Listened to What You Said and not What You Meant." Each of these advertisements includes visual effects along with playful puns which are left to the consumer to ponder. To some these taglines may be concrete; however, to others they may be ambiguous. The interpretation of these tropes may or may not have an impact on the success of said campaigns.

Consumers may love, hate, or be indifferent to various tropes. The primary purpose of this research is to discover how consumers' interpretations of tropes in advertising impact the success of the campaign.

Literature review

Within the past 20 years, advertisements have become less straightforward and more metaphorical; be it through pictures or words, most advertisements today present some form of trope (McQuarrie & Phillips, 2005). This tactic is prevalent in magazine advertisements. Examples of trope advertisements include taglines such as "smell like a man, man" (Old Spice), "you can't wait to get it on" (Trojan), and "There are some things money can't buy. For everything else, there's MasterCard" (Hershey). The explanation for this execution style is that advertisers believe that consumers are more receptive to metaphorical advertisements (McQuarrie & Phillips, 2005).

The purpose of this research is to (1) look deeper into how consumers process and react to tropes in advertising, (2) determine whether the perceived message of a consumer is what the advertiser was trying to convey and the importance of this understanding, and (3) introduce a new empirical framework which displays how consumers' interpretation of tropes impact the success of an advertising campaign.

How consumers process tropes

In order to successfully comprehend tropes in advertising, consumers must allow their mind to explore the underlying meaning which the advertiser is attempting to convey (Toncar & Munch, 2001). An example of this type of advertisement is Trojan's closing tagline "You can't wait to get it on." In this commercial, the advertiser is using

DOI: 10.1057/9781137492265.0013

a pun. They are referring to the sexual act as well as the product. Another example of trope advertising is in the Smart car ad. This trope is depicted solely through pictures. The image reveals a world of pollution through the windshield of the car, but where the wipers have cleaned is clear skies. The intended message is that people should drive the Smart because it is conducive to a less polluted environment. Ford also makes use of trope advertising in a print ad which uses an octopus as a car with the subheading stating "Great Grip Come Rain or Shine." Other trope-infused ads can be found in the appendix.

According to Toncar & Munch (2001) tropes in print advertising should have a higher positive effect on cognitive processing as well as memory and attitude toward the advertisement. It has also been proven that using tropes in advertising is an effective way to reach consumers who are rather disinterested. Advertising research has shown that the comprehension of tropes is prohibited by shallow information processing, which is a part of levels one and two of Mick's levels of subjective comprehension (Toncar & Munch, 2001). The benefit of shallow processing is that the explicit message lies within these two levels which thereby lead to the consumer concluding the intended message based on the explicit message provided in the copy. Because consumers are required to think on a deeper level when processing a trope, they may feel a great sense of accomplishment after successfully decoding the message, hence having a higher appreciation for the company for creating a cunning advertisement. The converse of trope advertising is that one may encounter those consumers who do not wish to attempt to cipher through the hidden meaning and just take the information for face value which may lead to a misunderstanding of the ad thereby causing the consumer to lose respect for the company because they do not comprehend the message.

There is controversy as to how consumers in high-involvement situations react to tropes versus how consumers in low-involvement situations interpret tropes. From one perspective, high-involvement situations are more favorable for trope advertising because the audience is in a heightened mode which causes them to be more receptive and participative with the advertisement. They are more likely to take the time to focus and interpret the trope. Conversely, other research shows that high-involvement situations are not suitable for trope advertising because they become distracted from the claim of

DOI: 10.1057/9781137492265.0013

the ad which causes the ad to lose its effectiveness (Petty & Cacioppo, 1983). When dealing with low-involvement situations, trope advertising is efficacious because the viewers are less interested in processing explicit messages. The added entertainment of a crafty trope grabs the attention of the viewer which increases the effectiveness of the ad (Toncar & Munch, 2001).

According to a study conducted by Toncar & Munch (2001), high-involvement consumers were more receptive to explicit messages versus tropes when focusing on claim type and attitude toward the product; however, there was no significant difference between those individuals who received tropes and those who received explicit messages when focusing on claim type and receiver's attitude. Low-involvement viewers were highly positively affected by tropes all around. Attitude toward products, receiver attitude, as well as depth of processing were positively correlated with trope advertising. Therefore, it is safe to conclude that when advertising to low-involvement audiences it is more effective to use tropes because it increases brand recognition and gives the consumer a positive outlook on the product.

Conceptual framework

As previously stated, this research is partially intended to introduce an innovative framework which will determine campaign success when using tropes. The RURRAL framework (as depicted in Figure6 .1) states that in order for a campaign to be deemed successful, the ad should evoke positive reactions, be uniquely understood, thus increasing brand recognition, product or brand recall, and hence purchase intentions.

Indicators of the RURRAL framework include tropes, metaphors, humor, puns, and pictorial depiction. The output from RURRAL includes attitude toward the ad, attitudes toward the brand, and purchase intent. Attitudes toward the ad as well as the brand can be positive or negative. The viewer may be more or less inclined to purchase the brand or product after viewing the ad.

A study was conducted using a sample of 63 people. Each individual viewed 5 trope advertisements and expressed on a scale of 1–5 with 1 being least positive and 5 being most positive, how each ad made them feel as well as their purchase intent.

DOI: 10.1057/9781137492265.0013

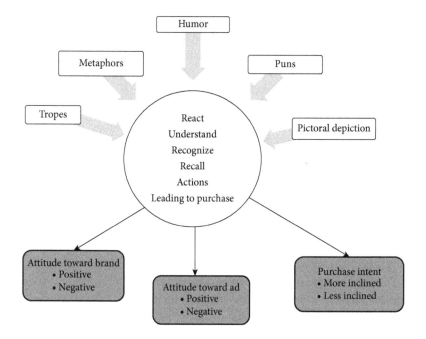

FIGURE 6.1   *RURRAL framework*

Data analysis

A focus group research was conducted where a sample size of 63 under-graduate students at a Historically Black College University (HBCU) were surveyed for the purpose of the research study, out of which 39 were women, 89 percent were aged between 21 and 30 years, 63.5 percent were Marketing and Management major students, even though students were from all different majors; 56 percent students were seniors and 32 percent were graduate students. In addition, 81 percent of students were African-Americans (see Table 6.1 for description of sample).

At first, the authors and a graduate assistant screened magazines and newspapers and got 20 ads. These 20 ads were presented to a group of four marketing professors. Among them, three were assistant professors and one was a lecturer who was teaching "Principle of Marketing." Five ads were finally selected and used in this research. These ads were put into an online survey and respondents were asked to read the ads and

DOI: 10.1057/9781137492265.0013

TABLE 6.1   *Description of sample*

Item	Classification	Percentage
Gender	Male	38.1
	Female	61.9
Age	21–25	73.0
	26–30	15.9
	31–35	3.2
	36–40	3.2
	46–50	1.6
	51–55	3.2
Area of specialization	Marketing	42.9
	Management	20.6
	Accounting	3.2
	CIS	1.6
	G-LIB	1.6
	General business	15.9
	Other	14.3
College standing	Sophomore	1.6
	Junior	9.5
	Senior	55.6
	Graduate student	31.7
	Other	1.6
Ethnicity	African-American	80.6
	White (Caucasian)	11.3
	Asian	1.6
	Native Hawaiian or other Pacific Islander	1.6
	Other	4.8

rate their feelings evoked by these ads and also their attitude toward the ad, attitude toward brands, and purchase intention.

We checked the correlations among the ad-evoked feelings and found that they are highly related. See Table 6.2 for correlations for feelings such as Worried–carefree, Insulted–honored, Indifferent–interested, Irritated–pleased, Depressed–cheerful, and Regretful–rejoicing. The correlations among them are between 0.653 and 0.875 and they are significant at the 0.01 level.

An exploratory principal component analysis with Varimax rotation was performed on the items of this semantic differential in order to reveal the basic dimensions of the feelings elicited. The result allowing the most homogeneous factor definition was obtained with a two-orthogonal factor solution, explaining 75 percent of the variance, which is shown in Table 6.3.

DOI: 10.1057/9781137492265.0013

TABLE 6.2 Correlation between ad-evoked feelings (1=strongest negative feeling; 7=strongest positive feeling)

Correlations		Worried–carefree	Insulted–honored	Indifferent–interested	Irritated–pleased	Depressed–cheerful	Regretful–rejoicing
Worried–carefree	Pearson correlation	1					
	Sig. (1-tailed)						
	Covariance	2.633					
Insulted–honored	Pearson correlation	0.734**	1				
	Sig. (1-tailed)	0.000					
	Covariance	1.745	2.149				
Indifferent–interested	Pearson correlation	0.651**	0.742**	1			
	Sig. (1-tailed)	0.000	0.000				
	Covariance	1.610	1.657	2.321			
Irritated–pleased	Pearson correlation	0.736**	0.792**	0.770**	1		
	Sig. (1-tailed)	0.000	0.000	0.000			
	Covariance	1.862	1.810	1.829	2.429		
Depressed–cheerful	Pearson correlation	0.771**	0.786**	0.663**	0.815**	1	
	Sig. (1-tailed)	0.000	0.000	0.000	0.000		
	Covariance	1.870	1.721	1.508	1.897	2.232	
Regretful–rejoicing	Pearson correlation	0.768**	0.803**	0.717**	0.787**	0.853**	1
	Sig. (1-tailed)	0.000	0.000	0.000	0.000	0.000	
	Covariance	1.793	1.694	1.571	1.765	1.834	2.071

Note: **Correlation is significant at the 0.01 level (1-tailed).
1=strongest negative feeling; 7=strongest positive feeling.

DOI: 10.1057/9781137492265.0013

TABLE 6.3   *Summary of exploratory factor analysis results for ad-evoked feelings*

Rotated component matrix	Component	
	1	2
Worried–carefree	0.463	*0.732*
Nervous–calm	0.366	*0.802*
Contemplative–impulsive	0.424	*0.756*
Critical–accepting	0.404	*0.845*
Cautious–adventurous	0.437	*0.793*
Dubious–confident	0.418	*0.789*
Pessimistic–hopeful	0.396	*0.816*
Callous–affectionate	*0.825*	0.380
Bad–good	*0.706*	0.574
Sad–happy	*0.779*	0.510
Insulted–honored	*0.856*	0.436
Indifferent–interested	*0.720*	0.488
Irritated–pleased	*0.766*	0.434
Unemotional–sentimental	*0.773*	0.361
Depressed–cheerful	*0.876*	0.378
Regretful–rejoicing	*0.832*	0.437
Eigenvalues	11.996	1.093
% of variance	74.975	6.833
Cronbach alpha	0.969	0.966

Extraction method: Principal component analysis.
Rotation method: Varimax with Kaiser normalization.
Rotation converged in three iterations.

KMO and Bartlett's test

Kaiser–Meyer–Olkin measure of sampling adequacy		0.924
Bartlett's test of sphericity	Approx. Chi-Square	1.437E3
	df	120
	Sig.	0.000

We also run the reliability analysis for attitude toward ads, attitude toward brands, and purchase intention. The Cronbach's alphas for these three constructs are 0.811, 0.931, and 0.841 (see Table 6.4). According to Hair, Anderson, Tatham, & Black (1998), the reliability of the construct is acceptable if Cronbach's alpha exceeds 0.70 and item-to-total correlations have greater than 0.50.

DOI: 10.1057/9781137492265.0013

TABLE 6.4   *Summary of confirmatory factor analysis results for A_{ad}, A_b, and PI*

Construct	Indicators	Cronbach alpha
A_{ad}	1. I like this ad a lot.	0.811
	2. I don't think this ad is interesting.	
	3. I think this ad is very convincing.	
	4. This ad is very appealing.	
	5. This ad is easy to forget.	
	6. This ad is not effective.	
A_b	7. Do you like the advertised brand?	
	8. Do you think this is a good brand?	0.931
	9. Do you feel favorably toward this brand?	
	10. Would you recommend the advertised brand to others?	
PI	11. I would not consider trying this brand.	0.841
	12. If I ran across this brand in a shop, I would buy it.	
	13. Do you feel favorably toward this brand?	
	14. When buying the advertised product, I would choose for another brand.	
	15. When buying the advertised product, I shall probably buy the advertised brand.	

The next step was to run a structural equation model to test the relationship among ad-evoked feelings and attitudes toward ads, attitudes toward brand, and purchase intention. We first run a correlation matrix which is shown in Table 6.5. From Table 6.5, we can see that ad-evoked feeling 1 is significantly positive related to attitudes toward ads, attitudes toward brand, and purchase intention.

Discussion

The RURRAL framework, which stands for react, understand, recognize, recall, and actions leading to purchase, is intended to determine if a campaign is successful when using tropes. From our analysis, these ads evoked two kinds of feelings, which are different from what Geuens (1998) found. A structural equation model will be used to examine the relations between the feelings and attitudes toward ads, attitudes toward brands, and purchase intention. But the correlation matrix shows that the ad-evoked feeling 1 is significantly positive related to all of these

DOI: 10.1057/9781137492265.0013

TABLE 6.5 *Correlations among ad-evoked feelings and attitudes toward ads, brand, and purchase intention*

	Mean	SD		Feeling 1	Feeling 2	A_{ad}	A_b	PI
Ad-evoked feeling 1	0		Pearson correlation	1				
			Sig. (2-tailed)					
		1.00	Covariance	1.000				
Ad-evoked feeling 2	0		Pearson correlation	0.000	1			
			Sig. (2-tailed)	1.000				
		1.00	Covariance	0.000	1.000			
A_{ad}	14.751		Pearson correlation	0.381^{**}	0.038	1		
			Sig. (2-tailed)	0.002	0.767			
		3.721	Covariance	1.437	0.145	13.876		
A_b	10.374		Pearson correlation	0.459^{**}	0.232	0.694^{**}	1	
			Sig. (2-tailed)	0.000	0.069	0.000		
		3.075	Covariance	1.382	0.699	7.954	9.457	
PI	12.601		Pearson correlation	0.396^{**}	0.028	0.777^{**}	0.813^{**}	1
			Sig. (2-tailed)	0.001	0.831	0.000	0.000	
		3.301	Covariance	1.303	0.091	9.555	8.251	10.900

Note: **Correlation is significant at the 0.01 level (2-tailed).

DOI: 10.1057/9781137492265.0013

three constructs, which is consistent with what we are trying to explore in this research.

Conclusion

The past 10 years have shown significant changes in the advertising industry. With tropes being a fairly new technique in advertising, it has become increasingly popular among advertisers. Studies have shown that among audiences with low involvement, tropes are effective in increasing brand recognition. These audiences are also more likely to recall ads with tropes. Conversely, high-involvement audiences often miss the intended message of the advertisement and therefore lose respect for the brand. However, using tropes with high-involvement audiences has no effect on the viewer's attitude and decoding the intended message. Tropes are an effective technique for advertising campaigns when targeted toward the correct audience.

References

Braun-Latour K. A., & Zaltman G. (2006). Memory Change: An Intimate Measure of Persuasion. *Journal of Advertising Research,* 57–72.

Hair, J. F., Anderson, R. E., Tatham, R. L., & Black, W. C. (1998). *Multivariate Data Analysis.* Prentice Hall. Upper Saddle River, NJ, 730.

McQuarrie E. F., & Phillips B. J. (2005). Indirect Persuasion in Advertising: How Consumers Process Metaphors Presented in Pictures and Words. *Journal of Advertising,* 7–20.

Mothersbaugh D. L., Huhmann B. A., & Franke G. R. (2002). Combinatory and Separative Effects of Rhetorical Figures on Consumers' Effort and Focus in Ad Processing. *Journal of Consumer Research,* 589–602.

Petty, R. E., Cacioppo, J. T., & Schumann, D. (1983). Central and Peripheral Routes to Advertising Effectiveness: The Moderating Role of Involvement. *Journal of Consumer Research,* 135–146.

DOI: 10.1057/9781137492265.0013

Toncar M., & Munch J. M. (2001). Consumer Responses to Tropes in Print Advertising. *Journal of Advertising*, 55–65.

Toncar M. F., & Munch J. M. (2003). The Influence of Simple and Complex Tropes on Believability, Importance and Memory. *Journal of Marketing Theory and Practice*, 39–53.

DOI: 10.1057/9781137492265.0013

7

How "True" Are Stereotypes? The Role of Stereotypes in Advertising

Grace Curry, Ulysses Brown, III, Jun Wu and Anshu Saxena Arora

▶

Abstract: *Advertising aims to adapt to the ever-changing consumer perceptions of all races, sexes, ethnicities, and attitudes of consumers worldwide. Yet to date there are still advertisements that portray persons of color either in a stereotypical manner or as background to European Americans. This research study explores and investigates the role of advertising in targeting African-American consumers through stereotypes and further examines the following questions. Do the stereotypes project the true feelings of African-American population? Should advertisers be held responsible for the continued perpetuation of the stereotypes?*

Keywords: advertisement; gender; minorities; race; stereotypes

Arora, Anshu Saxena and Sabine Bacouël-Jentjens. *Advertising Confluence: Transitioning Marketing Communications into Social Movements.* New York: Palgrave Macmillan, 2015. DOI: 10.1057/9781137492265.0014.

DOI: 10.1057/9781137492265.0014

Introduction

The racial and ethnic composition of America has changed considerably from a decade ago. And this composition is going to continue to change decades into the future. With the influx of immigrants from all over the globe, America is becoming browner. Yet, it does not seem as though many advertisers are paying close attention to this undeniable fact. Although the representation of ethnic groups in advertisements has increased in recent years (Zinkhan, Qualls, & Biswas, 1988), it is still not enough. There are still less representations of people of color in television and magazine advertisements. And when people of color are represented there is a hint of covert stereotyping.

Stereotyping is a psychological categorization of specific social groups held by the general public which influences decision-making and information-processing tasks (Gaertner & McLaughlin, 1983; Greenwald & Banaji, 1995).

African-Americans currently face the same stereotypes from times passed. Many African-Americans in television advertisements are seen, but not heard. However, when they are heard they share the advertisement with a white counterpart. This is noteworthy; television advertisements merit particular attention because they are key components of television, and because as Entman & Rojecki (2000) contended, they are "indicators of the culture's racial heartbeat" (p. 162), representing both cultural norms but also having the potential to improve racial relations (Henderson & Baldasty, 2003).

Advertisers may not realize how important of a role they play when it comes to stereotyping African-Americans, and are not intentionally producing stereotypical advertisements. Their goal is to get information out about a product or service to their market segment. But advertisers need to pay attention to who they are marketing to, and let their market segment assist with determining if a particular print or commercial may be perceived as stereotypical, especially if the market segmentation is African-American. Advertisers have a strong influence on shaping the perceptions of people, based on how characters in the advertisements are portrayed. Furthermore, advertisements either have the ability to help eradicate the negative perceptions of African-Americans, or they can facilitate pervasive stereotypes, which may increase racism. There is also more at risk.

Negative stereotypes of African-American in advertising may affect the self-esteem of African-Americans. The continuation of minimal

DOI: 10.1057/9781137492265.0014

representation or negative depictions of oneself reflected in media may cause many African-Americans to question their self-worth and importance to society. More importantly, these destructive images or lack thereof affect African-American children exponentially, since African-American children watch considerably more television than Caucasian children (Slaughter, 2003). It is also important to note that children cannot fully differentiate what is fact and what is fiction when watching television. Advertisers must realize that more is at stake than selling a product or service.

In this research study the stereotyping of African-Americans in advertisements will be explored. This stereotyping not only affects African-Americans, but all Americans as a whole. The goal of this research is to examine how advertising stereotypes propagate racism and its effects on society and determine if advertisers share a responsibility in the perpetuation of stereotypes or if they are simply providing Americans with what they want.

Literature review

Stereotypes

Gaertner & McLaughlin (1983), Bodenhausen (1988), Greenwald & Banaji (1995), as stated earlier, have defined stereotyping as a psychological categorization of specific social groups held by the general public which influences decision-making and information-processing tasks. Stereotyping has been further dichotomized into polarized appraisal theory (Linville, 1982; Linville & Jones, 1980) or in-group bias theory (Brewer, 1979; Wilder, 1981). These theories assume that people categorized individuals on whether they belong to the in-group or out-group (Qualls & Moore, 1990). In-groups are those that look like the persons doing the categorization and out-groups are those that look dissimilar to the person doing the categorization.

African-American stereotypes have been studied for many decades. Shuey, King, & Griffith (1953) reported that 0.6 percent of African-Americans were in advertisements, 95.3 percent of the time they were represented as unskilled laborers, entertainers, or athletes. Kern-Foxworth (1994) expressed that people of color are frequently not present; when they are, it is often in marginal or stereotypical roles. One may wonder how the absence of African-Americans may lead to stereotypes. One explanation is dominant group ideology.

DOI: 10.1057/9781137492265.0014

Hirschman (1993: 537) defined ideology as a widely shared "system of beliefs that emanate from the promulgate," a certain worldview and that ideology means by which dominant groups sustain and dominate their power over other groups. It is possible to communicate dominant group ideology through media. Duckitt (1992) states that media can communicate racial prejudice in a number of ways, including omission (i.e., ignoring the existence of African-Americans), stereotyping, and showing African-Americans in disproportionate number of "bad" or low-status roles. As Bristor, Lee, & Hunt (1995) stated, it is important to bring attention to these types of covert and possible unintentional negative portrayals of African-Americans in order to readdress race-based inequalities.

All images of African-Americans can shape and strengthen postulations of those who have limited interactions with them. And if more negative portrayals are presented via advertisements, stereotypes of African-Americans will persist. In order to prevent these negative assumptions, Bristor, Lee, & Hunt (1995) suggest African-Americans should be portrayed in roles other than successful athletes, but also in high-status roles, such as managers and other professionals.

Another apprehension that should be expressed is the possible loss of revenue advertisers may undergo from the African-American community. African-Americans, like any other population, are more likely to purchase products or services from companies that have persons in advertisements that look like them. African-American buying power has increased 166 percent from 1990 to 2007 compared to a 124 percent in White buying power (Selig Center, 2007). Therefore, it also seems plausible that the commercial messages should not contain any negative stereotypes.

The purpose of this chapter is to examine exactly what type of damage may come about due to advertising stereotypes of African-Americans. Additionally, this research will answer the following questions:

▸ Do the stereotypes project the true feelings of the African-American population?
▸ Are these types of stereotypical advertisements harmful to the self-esteem of people of color and how do these perceptions affect different ethnicities including gender?

DOI: 10.1057/9781137492265.0014

▸ Should advertisers be held responsible for the continued perpetuation of the stereotypes?

Conceptual framework

The Stereotypes Hypothesis Model expounds upon the relationship between stereotypes, ad-evoked feelings, attitudes toward ads, attitudes toward brands, and purchase intentions. Figure7 .1 demonstrates the conceptual framework. The conceptualization is that there is a direct relationship of stereotypes with ad-evoked feelings, attitude toward the ad, and attitude toward the brand, which all will affect current or future intentions to purchase a product.

Research methodology

The research methodology includes two stages.

Qualitative stage: Ten health and fashion magazines (Seventeen, Shape, Men's Health, Women's Health, Oprah, Allure, Elle, Details, Lucky, and Cosmopolitan) were examined, which resulted in 60 advertisements. These 60 ads/stimuli were presented to a panel of 21 students and five faculty members. The purpose of this qualitative stage was to determine which ads contained negative stereotypical portrayals of African-Americans. The occurrences of negative stereotypical portrayals were

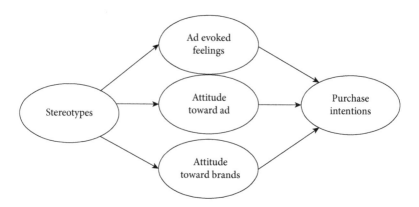

FIGURE 7.1   *Stereotypes' conceptual framework*

DOI: 10.1057/9781137492265.0014

counted and gave rise to five ads/stimuli that were nominated—one of an African-American male portrayed in a marginal role, two of African-American women in erotic roles, and two of African-American women in overexaggerated portrayals.

Quantitative stage: These five ads were formulated into an online survey to measure attitudes and behaviors among males and females. A sample of 72 students from a Historically Black College University (HBCU) was surveyed for the purpose of this research. The five ads were given to students in random order to avoid any bias. The population at a HBCU is mostly homogenous with parallel sociodemographic backgrounds. Gender was included as a cataloging question. The findings from this research were indiscriminate for males versus females. Out of the 72 students 60 percent were women and 81.9 percent were African-American, and 9.7 percent were Caucasian American. Table 7.1 provides details of the sample.

A one-way analysis of variance was conducted to explore the impact of positive and negative cultural meanings on gender, as shown in Table 7.2. Figure7 .2 shows the cultural ad-interpretation differences between males

TABLE 7.1   *Gender, age, and ethnicity of the sample*

		Frequency	Percent	Valid percent	Cumulative percent
Gender					
Valid	Male	29	40.3	40.3	40.3
	Female	43	59.7	59.7	100.0
	Total	72	100.0	100.0	
Age					
Valid	21–25	50	69.4	69.4	69.4
	26–30	14	19.4	19.4	88.9
	31–35	6	8.3	8.3	97.2
	36–40	2	2.8	2.8	100.0
	Total	72	100.0	100.0	
Ethnicity					
Valid	African-American	59	81.9	84.3	84.3
	White (Caucasian)	7	9.7	10.0	94.3
	Asian	1	1.4	1.4	95.7
	Native Hawaiian or other Pacific Islander	1	1.4	1.4	97.1
	Other	2	2.8	2.9	100.0
	Total	70	97.2	100.0	
Missing	system	2	2.8		
Total	72		100.0		

DOI: 10.1057/9781137492265.0014

TABLE 7.2 *ANOVA*

		Sum of squares	df	Mean square	F	Sig.
Does the ad provide a different but POSITIVE meaning when applied to different (your) culture/subculture?	Between groups	3.691	1	3.691	3.226	0.077
	Within groups	78.956	69	1.144		
	Total	82.648	70			
Does the ad provide a different but NEGATIVE meaning when applied to different (your) culture/subculture?	Between groups	11.726	1	11.726	13.436	0.000
	Within groups	60.218	69	0.873		
	Total	71.944	70			
View the ad again, at least view it three more times—on repeated viewings, do you encounter different POSITIVE messages?	Between groups	7.290	1	7.290	8.029	0.006
	Within groups	62.654	69	0.908		
	Total	69.944	70			
View the ad again, at least view it three more times—on repeated viewings, do you encounter different but NEGATIVE messages?	Between groups	11.060	1	11.060	13.201	0.001
	Within groups	57.813	69	0.838		
	Total	68.873	70			

DOI: 10.1057/9781137492265.0014

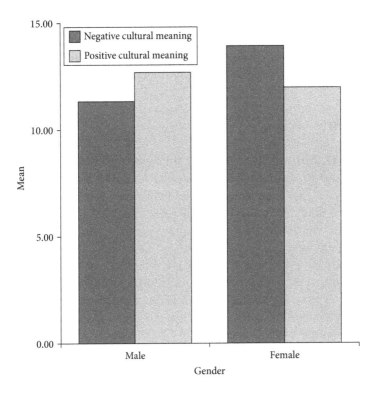

FIGURE 7.2 *Gender-based cultural ad-interpretation differences*

and females. Stereotypes generate different responses among males and females, as shown in Table 7.2 and Figure7 .2.

Research findings

After conducting the research, it was found that women viewed the advertisements depicting African-Americans one time as having a more negative cultural meaning and less positive cultural meaning than men. After viewing the ads multiple times, women were least likely to see positive cultural meaning in the advertisement than men. However, upon further viewing women perceived more negative meaning from the advertisements. This means that stereotypes disturb women more

DOI: 10.1057/9781137492265.0014

than men. Positive meanings from an advertisement and brand may lead to brand interest and an optimistic intent to purchase. However, advertisements that represents brands that are perceived as having negative meaning will not lead to positive intentions to purchase.

Conclusion

The purpose of this study is to examine the types of damage that may come about due to advertising stereotypes of African-Americans. The proposed "stereotypes" conceptual model may be accepted to explain that perceived stereotypes affect African-Americans' feelings about an advertisement, which leads to attitudes about the brand and intentions to purchase a product.

The research findings from this study are significant with respect to the use of positive/negative synchronic polysemy and positive/negative diachronic polysemy to determine positive intent of purchase. There are a few limitations with this research that should be discussed. First, a convenient sample of 72 students from a HBCU was surveyed and the majority of the students were African-American. Therefore, the sample size was not representative. Second, there were limitations with the advertisements chosen. Out of the five selected advertisements, four were portrayals of women. And full depictions of all possible African-American stereotypes were not examined.

These finding reflect similar results from previous research. African-Americans are aware and affected by negative portrayal in advertisement and yet advertisers still use them. One reason may be that those making decisions about the advertisements are not African-Americans and may not see the advertisements as stereotypical portrayals. Another indication is that African-Americans are seen as a homogenous group that only responds to broad advertisements. Implications from this study demonstrate that more realistic advertisements of African-Americans in roles other than stereotypical depictions are needed. For instance, more advertisements of African-Americans as managers, bank tellers, teachers, and doctors, are necessary to reflect more accurate portrayals of the group. Future research may focus on the reasons why women are affected by stereotypical portrayals in advertisements more than men. Additionally, more research should be conducted to determine why

DOI: 10.1057/9781137492265.0014

advertisers continue to use stereotypical advertisements of African-Americans.

References

Bandura A. (1977). *Social Learning Theory*. Oxford: Prentice-Hall, Print.

Brewer M. B. (1979). In-group Bias in the Minimal Intergroup Situation: A Cognitive-Motivational Analysis. *Psychology Bulletin*, 86(2), 307–324.

Bristor J. M., Lee R. G., & Hunt M. R. (1995). Race and Ideology: African American Images in Television Advertising. *Journal of Public Policy & Marketing*, 14(1), 48–59.

Duckitt J. (1992). *The Social Psychology of Prejudice*. New York: Praeger Press.

Entman R., & Rojecki A. (2000). The Black Image in the White Mind: Media and Race in America. Chicago: University of Chicago Press.

Gaertner S. L., & McLaughlin J. P. (1983). Racial Stereotypes: Associations and Ascriptions of Positive and Negative Characteristics. *Social Psychology*, 56, 5–18.

Greenwald A. G., & Banaji M. R. (1995). Implicit Social Cognition: Attitudes, Self-Esteem, and Stereotypes. *Psychology Review*, 102, 4–27.

Henderson J. J., & Baldasty G. J. (2003). Race, Advertising, and Prime-Time Television. *The Howard Journal of Communications*, 14(2), 97–112.

Hirschman E. C. (1993). Ideology in Consumer Research, 1980 and 1990: A Marxist and Feminist Critique. *Journal of Consumer Research*, 19, 537–555.

Kern-Foxworth, M. (1994). *Aunt Jemima, Uncle Ben and Rastus: Blacks in Advertising, Yesterday, Today and Tomorrow*. Westport, CT: Greenwood Press.

Linville P. W. (1982). The Complexity-Extremity Effect and Age-Based Stereotyping. *Journal of Personality and Social Psychology*, 42(2), 193–211.

Linville P. W., & Jones E. (1980). Polarized Appraisal of Out-Group Members. *Journal of Personality and Social Psychology*, 38(5), 689–703.

Qualls W. J., & Moore D. J. (1990). Stereotyping Effects on Consumers' Evaluation of Advertising: Impact of Racial Differences between Actors and Viewers. *Psychology & Marketing*, 7(2), 135–151.

DOI: 10.1057/9781137492265.0014

Selig Center. (2007). The Multicultural Economy 2007. Atlanta: University of Georgia Press.

Shuey A. M., King A., & Griffith B. (1953). Stereotyping Negroes and Whites: An Analysis of Magazine Pictures. *Public Opinion Quarterly*, 17 (Summer), 281–287.

Slaughter E. (2003). Survey of Children's Health and Obesity in America. *Prevention Magazine*.

Stevenson T. H., & Swayne L. E. (1999). The Portrayal of African-Americans in Business-to-Business Direct Mail: A Benchmark Study. *Journal of Advertising*, 28 (3), 25–35.

Taylor C. R., & Lee J. Y. (1995). Portrayals of African-American, Hispanic, and Asian Americans in Magazine Advertising. *American Behavioral Scientist*, 38(4), 608–621.

Watson S., Dejong P. E., & Slack J. L. (2009). Impact of Racial Attitudes on Consumers' Evaluation of Black Character Advertisements: Does Spokesperson skin Color Make a Difference? *Communication Research Reports*, 26(2), 91–104.

Wilder D. A. (1981). Perceiving Persons as Group: Categorization and Intergroup Relations. In D. L. Hamilton (Ed.), *Cognitive Process in Stereotyping in Intergroup Behavior*. Hillsdale, NJ.

Zinkhan G., Qualls W. J., & Biswas A. (1988). The Racial Composition of Domestic Advertising: A Longitudinal Analysis of Blacks in Magazines and Television. Working Paper, University of Houston.

DOI: 10.1057/9781137492265.0014

8

The Value of Social Networks in the World of Advertising

April Harris and Reginald Leseane

Abstract: *Since the inception of the Internet, firms have developed strategies to incorporate the Web in their business models. Most recently, the explosion of social networking sites has changed the business world. This study looks into the phenomenon of social networks and its impact on advertising. Firms are gravitating toward social networking sites to reach target markets, create brand awareness, promote positive attitudes toward their brand names and develop brand trust. This study will investigate how social networking sites can be used as a marketing tool and how social networks can assist marketers in identifying and communicating with target markets.*

Keywords: advertising; brand attitude; brand awareness; brand trust; social networks; target markets; WOM

Arora, Anshu Saxena and Sabine Bacouël-Jentjens. *Advertising Confluence: Transitioning Marketing Communications into Social Movements.* New York: Palgrave Macmillan, 2015. DOI: 10.1057/9781137492265.0015.

Introduction

The evolution of technology continues to change and challenge the business environment. The world of advertising is no exception. In 2000, 44.1 percent of the US population was using the Internet. By 2010, that number increased to 77.3 percent (internetworldstats.com, 2011), demonstrating a 33 percent increase in 10 years. As Internet use increases, the type of Internet use continues to evolve. Today's new development is online social networking sites. Social networking sites are defined as web-based services that allow individuals to construct a public or semipublic profile within a bounded system; articulate a list of other users with whom they share a connection; and view and traverse their list of connections and those made by others within the system (Boyd & Ellison, 2007). Social networks are made up of users and their relationships. Most online social networks allow members to post profiles, connect to friends and family, maintain friendships, and invite others to join, creating a complex virtual network of communication (Wasserman & Faust, 1994). The business world is becoming more knowledgeable about the potential benefits these social networking sites hold for them. The constant growth in Internet users and the expansion of use throughout the population show that it is inevitable for firms to include online advertising in their marketing strategy, especially within social networking sites.

As technology evolves, people are spending more and more time online for daily functions whether at work or at home. A 2005 study by the University of South California showed that 78.6 percent of Americans go online, averaging 13.3 hours of use a week (www.TMCnet.com, 2006). Figure 8.1 lists Internet users by age group. This growth of Internet use in society creates a shift in how firms need to reach their target customers and consumer markets. Traditional forms of advertising are slowly becoming obsolete. Firms must develop strategies that will enable them to identify and reach those users who are moving away from reading the newspapers, watching television, etc. Firms must research and investigate online activities to reach their customer base. Consumers are now empowered with more knowledge about products and companies and advertising has lost much of its well-established route of influence (Săvulescu, 2011). Firms with a strong network base will dominate the market and increase revenues (Arthur, 1996). In order to ensure that

DOI: 10.1057/9781137492265.0015

Age	Pct of Americans in age group online (%)
12–17	87
18–24	82
25–29	85
30–34	83
40–44	76
45–49	73
50–54	68
55–59	68
60–64	55
65–69	57
70–75	26
76+	17

FIGURE 8.1   *Age of Internet users*

Source: Wash Post 2/6/06 quoting Pew Internet & American Life Project surveys conducted Oct.–Nov. 2004 (teens) and Jan.–June 2005 (adults)

marketers are successfully reaching their target markets, firms must invest in online advertising.

Brand communities are specialized, non-geographically bound communities based on a structured set of social relationships among brand admirers (Muniz & O'Guinn, 2001). Social networking sites provide the ideal platform for these types of communities to exist. Social networks allow firms to establish profiles where consumers can opt to be associated with specific brands and have the ability to display links to those brands or to information about those brands on their own profiles. Marketers are able to publish product information and updates, and product owners are able to communicate with one another and the firm; social communication is king in brand communities. Consumers are now able to give feedback and provide opinions on demand. Communication is constant, with no time restraints, allowing information seekers to obtain required information 24 hours a day. Brand communities are

DOI: 10.1057/9781137492265.0015

resources for both the customer and the firm by allowing each to connect with others and obtain required information.

The goal of this study is to determine if social networking sites assist marketers in identifying and communicating with target markets. The research will also determine if participation in online social network sites, thereby creating brand communities, has an impact on brand trust, attitude, and awareness. This research addresses the following questions:

▶ Does positive social communication create positive brand trust and attitude, while negative social communication creates negative brand trust and attitude?
▶ Does participation in social networks increase brand awareness?
▶ Do social networks aid marketers in identifying and communicating with target markets?

Literature review

Online advertising got its start in 1994, just after the rise of the Internet. There are various forms of online advertising that include e-mail, banner messages, click-through, etc. Firms have invested a large percentage of their marketing budgets to online advertising. Online advertisements generate visits to a firm's individual website, increase online and offline sales, and contribute to brand awareness. Revenue for online advertising grew tremendously from 1996 to 2000. In 2000, online advertising spending in the United States was at $8.2 billion (IAB, 2000). Growth leveled off in 2000. Online revenue declined in 2001–2002, then began to climb again in 2003. Hollis (2005) stated that a revived US economy, industry maturity, and continued evidence of advertising success aided in this 2003 improvement. Firms began to understand that people were using the web to research products and decide on their next purchase. All online research does not lead to online purchases but can lead to future in-store purchases. Eighty-nine percent of consumers pre-shop online, which suggests that online advertising drives in-store revenues (Sathish, Prem Kumar, & Bharath, 2011). Search engines and social networks receive the majority of their revenues from advertisement. Advertisement is the primary source of revenue for social networking sites. Google reported advertising revenue of $1.578 billion in September 2005, while MySpace reported $440 million in advertising revenue in

DOI: 10.1057/9781137492265.0015

2007 (Cha, 2009). This study focuses on online advertising within social networking sites only, with a primary focus on Facebook as the leading social networking site.

Social networks and brand awareness

Social networks have been around since the beginning of human existence as people worked together to survive and, ultimately, to thrive. Throughout the years, people have formed social networks with family, friends, coworkers, etc., so the concept of social networks is not new. In contrast, online social networking sites are a new phenomenon. In recent times, social networking sites have become increasingly popular because of their ability to connect people with common interests throughout the world (Acar & Polonsky, 2007). With its increased number of users, these social networks have the potential to provide profitable benefits to companies, making social networking sites a new platform for marketing. For example, in 2009, Facebook reported having more than 307 million users worldwide, while, by comparison, MySpace, a second networking site, reported having 123 million (Albanesius, 2009). Today there are more than 800 million active Facebook users (www.facebook.com, 2011). MySpace reportedly has 33.1 million active users today (http:// en.wikipedia.org/wiki/Myspace, 2011), a significant decrease from 2009, moving MySpace from the number one visited social networking site to 91. Facebook has superseded MySpace in number of users and has become the dominant social networking site.

Facebook was launched in February 2004 and became very popular over a short time span (Săvulescu, 2011). Research shows that Facebook is the ideal marketing platform with (1) its significant user base; (2) the time users spend on Facebook, due to its entertainment and functionality; and (3) its continuous flow of new features and services (Alba & Stay, 2008). Members use the social networking site to reconnect with past friends, coworkers, lost loved ones, and family members. It allows people to interact, socialize, and keep in touch no matter where they are. Facebook statistics note that more than 50 percent of active users log onto Facebook in any given day (www.facebook.com, 2011). Social networking websites, such as Facebook, have created forums for firms to join and reach their customer base. Firms have the ability to create company profiles, such as "Pages" (i.e., Fanpages) or "Groups" on Facebook. Firms are allowed to participate in the social network site but are not allowed to

DOI: 10.1057/9781137492265.0015

be intrusive and pushy as some traditional advertising has the reputation of being. The primary difference in a Fanpage profile versus a personal profile is that company pages are not allowed to send out friend requests. This limitation allows Facebook to provide the brand with a presence, while respecting members' privacy and social environment.

Participating in social networks and establishing a presence in them provide firms the opportunity to promote brand awareness. Social networks allow members to visit a firm's Fanpage and "Like" the page or suggest the page to a friend. This process helps spread brand awareness throughout the network and allow those who want to receive product updates or information from a particular firm to do so. Those who are not interested in a particular brand are not burdened with pop-up messages, etc. This method of "come at your own will" has benefits for the firm as well. Instead of the traditional method of advertising to the masses, hoping to reach potential customers, firms have the ability to cater to those consumers who have expressed interest. Interested parties can then receive updates and notification from brands that they are truly interested in. Previous research has shown that continuous exposure increases a person's liking of an item and establishes a positive attitude toward a stimulus (Monroe, 1976), therefore concluding that continuous positive brand exposure not only enhances brand awareness, but promotes a positive attitude toward a brand. We will discuss attitude toward a brand later in this chapter. Given the above environment and data, one could logically surmise that social networks can be used to promote brand awareness. Therefore, the following hypothesis will be evaluated:

> H1: Participation in social networks is positively related to brand awareness.

Social communication, brand trust, and brand awareness

In this study, social communication is used to define all aspects of online communication between members, friends, brands, etc. performed within a social networking site such as Facebook. Social communication may take several forms, for example, posts, blogs, chats, IM, comments, likes, and dislikes. The most common forms of social communication are user-generated content (UGC) and word-of-mouth (WOM) communication. UGC is any material created and uploaded to the Internet by a nonmedia professional, such as a comment, video, picture (Sathish, et al., 2011). WOM is defined as an unpaid form of advertising, where

DOI: 10.1057/9781137492265.0015

satisfied (or unsatisfied) customers tell others how much they liked (or disliked) a company's product or service. Consumers are empowered by social communication and are more critical but also eager to receive and contribute information (Săvulescu, 2011). Research has shown that WOM is powerful within social networks and influences brand attitude and purchase decisions; if users decide to purchase a product they can influence their friends to purchase the product, increasing the possibility of sales (Ulusu, 2010). Seventy percent of consumers visited social media websites to get information, of which 49 percent made purchase decisions based on that information (DEI Worldwide, 2008). Consumers trust user-generated messages on social media over traditional mass media and are more likely to believe real experiences, accessed from online communities, than company-advertised media (Dennis, Morgan, Wright, & Jayawardhena, 2010; Chung & Austria, 2010). Brand communities have a positive effect on consumers' brand attitude and attachment (McAlexander, Schouten, & Koenig, 2002). The free, always available, UGC within these communities encourages positive brand attitude (Riegner, 2007). Consumers are positive about communicating with brands online and when they experience positive social advertising and valuable information, they are willing to take action and spread positive WOM about the brand (DEI Worldwide, 2008). A majority of users see online recommendations from others as valuable and credible, with 60 percent of social network users reporting that they were likely to pass along information they received online (DEI Worldwide, 2008). Thus, social communication has a strong influence over brand trust and attitude within social networking sites. Given the above discussion, the following hypothesis will be evaluated:

> H2: Social communication is a significant predictor of brand attitude and trust.

Social networks and target markets

Social network functionalities such as "Fanpages" and "Groups," mentioned earlier, can be utilized to identify a brand's target market. The benefit to the brand is that instead of seeking customers who are interested in their brand, those interested parties willingly come to them. Therefore, marketers tasked with identifying target markets must change their focus from simply identifying the target market to keeping the interested parties engaged in social media. Facebook members

DOI: 10.1057/9781137492265.0015

create profiles listing their interests, likes, dislikes, professions, favorite movies, music, etc., and Facebook allows members to group based on those similar characteristics. Information clustered in this way provides marketers with valuable information about a population that could later lead to identification of their target markets. Social networking sites provide brands the opportunity to comfortably approach consumers and specifically target them based on common characteristics or interests. Social networks can facilitate information between brands and members, but require involvement and activity from marketers (Sãvulescu, 2011). Social networks provide firms the ability to communicate with existing and potential customers through the creation of online brand communities.

Firms recognize that social networking sites allow them to create brand communities and that these web-enhanced brand communities lead to relationship-marketing communication (Ulusu, 2010). Through the use of groups and pages discussed above, social networks give brands the ability to develop a community where they are able to market to a specific group of potential consumers. These communities provide direct communication to consumers interested in specific products. They allow marketers to receive user feedback, provide connections to devoted users, and provide an avenue to present product information updates and recalls. Brand communities allow firms to distribute information quickly about products or new developments. Marketers are able to receive and respond to a customer's request quickly and obtain instant feedback. In addition to useful information, brand communities provide members with easy information exchange with other members, promote involvement through generation of ideas, and promote community participation that is not restricted by time or space (Palmer & Koenig-Lewis, 2009). Brand communities should be interactive and used as a way to maintain and enhance relationships with consumers (Chung & Austria, 2010). Social media has created a new type of consumer, one more engaged, interactive, and willing to communicate and create useful content for marketers (Sãvulescu, 2011). Given these findings, social networks assist with segmenting target markets and facilitating communication through the use of brand communities and the collection of member profile data. Thus, the following hypothesis will be examined:

> H3: Social networks will have a significant impact on identifying and communicating with target markets.

DOI: 10.1057/9781137492265.0015

Conceptual framework

A conceptual model (Figure 8.2) is used in this study to demonstrate the relationship between social networks/social communication and brand awareness, brand attitude, brand trust, and target markets, which ultimately leads to a successful social marketing strategy. This study introduces the SAM Conceptual Framework model. The SAM model is defined as the Socially Advertised Marketing model. This model is designed to emphasize social media and social communication and demonstrate their impact on key marketing concepts. In this study, the SAM model will illustrate the causal relationship and connections between social networks and social communication and show their effect on increasing brand awareness, promoting positive brand attitude, fostering brand trust, and identifying target markets, leading to the development of a brand-specific social marketing strategy. The SAM model shows how social networking sites provide the platform for brands to speak directly to consumers, allowing brands to understand what consumers want. Brands must engage in social conversation with consumers, avoiding product-focused conversations. Using the appropriate social etiquette, that is, avoiding conversations focused on specific products, is important in the social environment. Having the appropriate interactions and social conversation with consumers within a social networking site will establish the brand's community. This brand community helps marketers select and communicate with its target market. Once the brand community is established, marketers have the opportunity to establish brand awareness. Marketers must make consumers aware of their brand and what they have to offer by developing relationships with consumers. Brands need to create a company profile that is creative and inviting. When brands welcome open communication, feedback, and interaction with consumers, the interaction develops a positive image for the brand. Brands should listen to consumers, provide useful information, and be open to both positive and negative feedback. This openness helps shape the consumers' attitude toward the brand. When brands maintain established relationships with consumers, they promote brand trust.

The SAM model of advertising

In online social networking, consumers will look for ways to be involved with the specific brand and will solicit others to get involved. Brands

DOI: 10.1057/9781137492265.0015

should develop contests, incorporate consumer ideas into future products, create free giveaways, design exclusive specials for online community members only, etc. to keep consumers engaged. The SAM model in this study demonstrates how the use of social networking sites and social communications allows brands to create a brand community that will attract and identify their target market, create brand awareness, develop brand attitude, and establish brand trust, leading to an effective social marketing strategy. Existing research in the area of social media, social networks, social networking sites, social communication, brand awareness, brand trust, brand attitude, and target markets is the basis of this study. Thorough review and analysis were used to identify and consolidate research findings in the above areas. Those findings are discussed throughout this study. Exploratory findings were used to guide the development of the conceptual framework and the SAM model. Previous research supports the causal relationship depicted in the SAM model (see Figure 8.2).

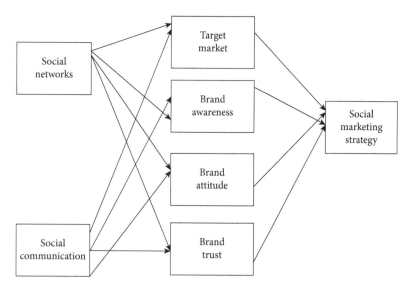

FIGURE 8.2   *The Socially Advertised Marketing model*

Source: Percentage of people who report the types of online sources they have visited to get information on a company, brand, or product (DEI, 2008).

DOI: 10.1057/9781137492265.0015

Managerial implications

Starbucks has received kudos from the marketing world on its efficient use of marketing within social networks, particularly Facebook. Starbucks is an example of a brand that can be said to have a firm understanding of the SAM concept and has mastered communication within Facebook. This brand knew that it was important to establish a presence within the leading social networking site and master the art of social communication. They realized that the standard form of marketing would not work in this particular medium. They developed a brand community within Facebook, creating a company profile that felt more personal than business-like. Starbucks shares thoughts and opinions on music, current events, sports, holidays, etc., through daily status updates. The company offers coupons, deals, and online exclusives, not just of their products, but also of other goods and services such as CDs. Starbucks trusts its members and believes in the level of service that it provides to its customers. This is evident in the decision to allow all UGC to be displayed on its home page as the default. This strategy is not something that a lot of brands opt to do; some companies delete negative comments, but Starbucks has chosen to do this as a measure of open communication. This approach instills trust in the consumers. The page is interactive; the company accepts and utilizes consumer feedback it receives from users within the social network and often rewards members with special deals online. Starbucks knows its target market and communicates well with them no matter the subject. It has fostered a positive brand attitude within users and developed trust for the brand. Starbucks has demonstrated that it is aware of the difference in marketing within social networking sites and has learned to be successful using guidelines and key concepts as those noted in the SAM model (Figure 8.2). Starbucks encourages user feedback and is very interactive with its community members; this communication demonstrates effective community management.

In contrast, Wal-Mart has not been so successful in implementing a social marketing strategy. Wal-Mart's attempts to enter the social networking world failed. Wal-Mart created a Facebook page but decided to limit the interactions available on the page to wall posts instead of allowing open user discussions. This strategy facilitated one-way communication, which is not favorable in a social networking environment. Some of the top reasons for joining a social network are to communicate

DOI: 10.1057/9781137492265.0015

and network. If a brand is not willing to provide open communication, it will never succeed in the social networking world. Wal-Mart entered the social environment attempting to use the same tactics used in traditional advertising, which is not feasible within social networking sites where the consumer has control. The focus must be directed to the consumer and not the product or service. Wal-Mart failed to establish relationships with consumers and it delivered poor social communication. When asked why it would not allow discussions on its page, the brand representative answered by stating that "the wall posts were the opportunity we decided to make available for online discussions." The brand failed to listen to the consumer, failed to understand the need for consumer involvement within the brand community, and delivered poor social communication as illustrated by the lack of concern displayed in this response. This approach ignited a host of negative comments about the brand. The company failed to recognize that the social environment is different and requires different advertising strategies than traditional advertisement. It did not establish relationships in order to build brand awareness, to develop positive brand attitude, or to establish trust with consumers. If Wal-Mart were to adopt the SAM model of advertising, it would be able to establish a successful social marketing strategy that could prove successful and allow it to establish and maintain consumer relationships.

The 2008 DEI study showed that more people visit social media websites to obtain brand information than any other online channel (see Figure 8.3). With the increased popularity of social networking sites, the mere presence of a brand in those communities promotes brand awareness. As mentioned, social networking sites afford brands the ability to develop brand communities, which provide the platform for brands to interact with consumers. Fanpages within social networking sites allow brands to establish a presence and nurture brand awareness. Maintaining interactive Fanpages in popular social networking sites will foment brand awareness. Social networks have forced marketers to understand that advertising should not be centered on the product or the brand, but must first focus on the customer, creating a brand–consumer engagement within a social network (Sǎvulescu, 2011). Sales follow relationships. To be effective firms must connect and establish relationships through the development of brand communities. The analysis of existing research supports hypothesis (H1), confirming that participation in social networks will increase brand awareness.

DOI: 10.1057/9781137492265.0015

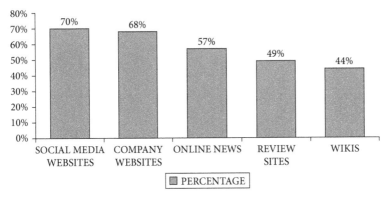

FIGURE 8.3   *Online sources visited for information*
Base: Among those who ever searched information online (DEI, 2008).

Positive social communication is the crux of success within social networks for positive brand trust and attitude. Research shows that brand trust and attitude is developed through social communication, primarily WOM and UGC. When people read about a brand or product within a social networking site, they place a high value on those comments. Research shows that 71 percent of users value recommendations and information received online (see Figure 8.4; DEI, 2008). On Facebook, when users receive suggestions to like a product, page, group, or brand, they typically do. This can lead users to view that brand's page or group, thus attracting new customers. Social communication exists on a brand's Fanpage or within brand-established Groups. Groups within social networking sites facilitate brand trust and attitudes. This type of user-promoted and -trusted marketing is valuable to a firm.

Consumers value online interactions with brands, with 67 percent of online searchers stating that they would likely pass along informa-tion they received online from brand representatives (DEI, 2008). If a firm wants to promote positive talk about its brand throughout a social network, it must communicate well with its existing and poten-tial customers. Firms must establish and maintain relationships with members in order to be accepted. Once accepted, members will suggest the brand to others, comment on the brand, post the brand on their personal profiles, etc., thereby promoting positive social communica-tion. This positive communication creates trust between the firm and

DOI: 10.1057/9781137492265.0015

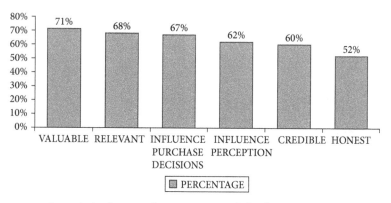

FIGURE 8.4   *Attitudes toward consumer-provided information*

its existing and potential customers. Users that experience positive communication with brands are more likely to spread positive WOM about that brand, value the information received, and take action, thus having a positive effect on brand attitude. Conversely, when customers feel invaded by the brand or believe that an advertisement is too aggressive for the social environment, they are likely to spread negative WOM which has a negative effect on brand attitude. Social communication, therefore, drives brand trust and attitude and supports our hypothesis (H2) that social communication has a significant impact and is positively related to brand trust and attitude.

Social networks provide propitious information such as member likes, dislikes, interests, professions, characteristics, demographic information, etc., all of which marketers seek to obtain. Research studies examined within the literature review substantiate that social networking sites provide brands with a database of information for marketing purposes. Firms are able to conduct market analysis, perform segmentations, and target specific members within a social networking site. Social networks offer firms the flexibility to use a variety of targeting strategies and to simultaneously implement multiple strategies, catering to the dynamics of various groups. While social networks can provide the apparatus to identify and communicate with a brand's target markets, marketers must know how to effectively communicate with consumers within social networking sites. Marketers must be creative and develop advertisements that do not feel like advertisements when communicating with their

DOI: 10.1057/9781137492265.0015

target market. In the world of social networking, conversation is the new advertising (Kotler, Kartajaya, & Setiawan, 2010). Firms must find ways to socialize with consumers, remembering not to be invasive, aggressive, or pushy. In a social network, that is not the type of communication people want to have. Marketers must understand that people are there to connect, not to be targeted. Communication with customers and potential customers should be about anything that interests the consumer or the popular topic of the day, not just about product information. If this is accomplished and incorporated into the firm's marketing strategy, the firm will be successful. Our hypothesis (H3) is supported and the answer to our question is yes, social networking sites can assist marketers in identifying and communicating with target markets.

Conclusion

This study will add to existing research on the topic of social media throughout the marketing industry. Future research will need to take a deeper look into the benefits of social networks on advertising. A longitudinal study is warranted to evaluate the long-term impact of social media on marketing, given various marketing strategies. Firms should be cautious about generalizing the results of this study, as this research is purely exploratory in nature. More quantitative research is needed in this area. Future quantitative research will be pursued to test and validate the SAM model introduced in this study.

This discussion provides useful insight for management and marketing professionals on the need to have social media at the core of their online marketing strategy. The study provides management with the framework to develop a cogent social marketing strategy, and the analysis provides details into the options available to firms within social networks. The study describes also the benefits of these options to the company, social etiquette requirements, the importance of brand communities, and the dominating factors that drive consumers. This method of marketing will prove beneficial to consumers because, as more brands adopt an effective social strategy, consumers will have access to more user-generated information and in-depth knowledge of products and services. Consumers will also benefit from valuable access to resources, from both users and the brands. This study supports the findings of previous research, concluding that social media marketing

DOI: 10.1057/9781137492265.0015

is pivotal to reaching consumers in today's society. No modern plan targeting users online is complete without a social network marketing component (Ulusu, 2010).

In conclusion, this study shows that social networks have changed the world of advertising by forcing marketers to think creatively using nontraditional methods. The constant stream of traffic makes involvement in social networks a must for firms, providing an unlimited amount of exposure with the potential to increase brand awareness, facilitate brand trust, and promote positive brand attitude and select target markets. The research concludes that social networks provide enormous value to the revitalized world of advertising and should be appropriately integrated into a firm's online marketing strategy.

References

Acar S. A., & Polonsky M. (2007). Online Social Networks and Insights into Marketing Communications. *Journal of Internet Commerce*, 6(4), 55–72.

Alba J., & Stay J. (2008). I'm on Facebook—Now What??? How to Get Personal, Business and Professional Value from Facebook. Cupertino, CA: *Happy About*.

Albanesius C. (2009). More Americans Go to Facebook Than MySpace, *PC Magazine*, June 16, http://www.pcmag.com/article2/0,2817,2348823,00.asp [Retrieved October 1, 2011].

Arthur W. B. (1996). Increasing Returns and the New World of Business. *Harvard Business Review*, 74 100–111.

Boyd D. M., & Ellison N. B. (2007). Social Network Sites: Definition, History, and Scholarship. *Journal of Computer-Mediated Communication* [online], 13(1) article 11. http://jcmc.indiana.edu/vol13/issue1/boyd.ellison.html [Retrieved September 26, 2011].

Cha J. (2009). Shopping on Social Networking Web Sites: Attitudes toward Real Versus Virtual Items. *Journal of Interactive Advertising*, 10(1), 77–93.

Chung C., & Austria K. (2010). Social Media Gratification and Attitude toward Social Media Marketing Messages: A Study of the Effect of Social Media Marketing Messages on Online Shopping Value. *Proceedings of the Northeast Business & Economics Association*, pp. 581–586.

DOI: 10.1057/9781137492265.0015

DEI Worldwide. (2008). Engaging Consumers Online. The Impact of Social Media on Purchasing Behavior; Volume One: Initial Findings United States 2008 [online]. http://www.deiworldwide.com/files/DEIStudy-Engaging%20ConsumersOnline-Summary.pdf [Retrieved September 25, 2011].

Dennis C., Morgan A., Wright L., & Jayawardhena C. (2010). The Influences of Social E-Shopping in Enhancing Young Women's Online Shopping Behaviour. *Journal of Customer Behaviour*, 9(2), 151–174.

Fulgoni G. M., & Mörn M. (2009). Whither the Click? How Online Advertising Works. *Journal of Advertising Research*, 49(2), 134–142.

Hollis N. (2005). Ten Years of Learning on How Online Advertising Builds Brands. *Journal of Advertising Research*, 45(2), 255–268.

IAB. (2000). Interactive Advertising Revenue Report 2000. PriceWaterhouseCoopers.

McAlexander J. H., Schouten J. W., & Koenig H. (2002). Building Brand Community. *Journal of Marketing*, 66(1), 38–54.

Monroe K. B. (1976). The Influence of Price Differences and Brand Familiarity on Brand Preferences. *Journal of Consumer Research*, 3 (1), 42–49.

Muniz Jr, A. M., & O'guinn, T. C. (2001). Brand community. *Journal of consumer research*, 27(4), 412–432.

Palmer A., & Koenig-Lewis N. (2009). An Experiential Social Network-Based Approach to Direct Marketing. *Direct Marketing: An International Journal*, 3 (3), 162–176.

Riegner C. (2007). Word of Mouth on the Web: The Impact of Web 2.0 on Consumer Purchase Decisions. *Journal of Advertising Research*, 47(4), 436–447.

Sathish M., Prem Kumar V. B., & Bharath S. (2011). Impacts of Online Advertising on Sales. *Journal of Marketing & Communication*, 7(1), 11–17.

Săvulescu R. (2011). Brand Talk on Facebook - a New Challenge in Marketing Communication. *Revista Romana de Comunicare si Relatii Publice*, 13(2), 19–30.

Ulusu Y. (2010). Determinant Factors of Time Spent on Facebook: Brand Community Engagement and Usage Types. *Journal of Yasar University*, 5(18), 2949–2957.

Wasserman S., & Faust K. (1994). *Social Network Analysis: Methods and Applications*.Cambridge: Cambridge University Press.

DOI: 10.1057/9781137492265.0015

www.entrepreneur.com/encyclopedia/term/82660.html [Retrieved November 4, 2011].

www.facebook.com (2011). Statistics, http://www.facebook.com/press/info.php?statistics [Retrieved October 1, 2011].

www.internetworldstats.com (2011). Internet Usage and Population Statistics for North America, http://www.internetworldstats.com/stats14.htm#north [Retrieved September 25, 2011].

www.TMCnet.com (2006). USC Study Finds Broadband to Be Most Popular Type of Internet Connection. (January 11, 2006) http://news.tmcnet.com/news/2006/jan/1277873.htm [Retrieved November 11, 2011].

www.wikipedia.com (2011). MySpace, http://en.wikipedia.org/wiki/Myspace [Retrieved October 1, 2011].

DOI: 10.1057/9781137492265.0015

Afterword

Lisa Yount

Promoting the Write Attitude through Student-Driven Research and Publication

The writing in this volume is innovative not only for the new ground it breaks in social movement advertising and marketing research, but also for the way that each piece of scholarship represents the close mentoring of a student author. Authentic teaching is the transmission of skills and expertise to a new generation so that they may enter and expand the discourse community of a field. The chapters in this publication exemplify the process of nurturing new perspectives and voices so that they may find expression and make significant contributions to knowledge production.

Savannah State University, the oldest public historically black university in the State of Georgia, develops productive members of a global society through high-quality instruction, scholarship, research, service, and community involvement. The University fosters engaged learning and personal growth in a student-centered environment that celebrates the African-American legacy while nurturing a diverse student body.

Reflective of our institutional identity and commitments, our signature university-wide writing initiative, *The Write Attitude*, is built on the following tenets:

Writing skills are essential for success and should evolve throughout our lifetime:

▸ Writing is a valuable tool for improving ourselves, our campus, our careers, and our communities.
▸ Writing skills must be attentively developed and reinforced, no matter what level of proficiency.
▸ Writing must be nurtured both inside and outside of the classroom to reinforce the practical role that writing will play in students' future professions.

Writing is foundational for the improvement of cognitive capacities:

▸ Writing contributes to critical thinking, reading comprehension, and mastery of academic content.
▸ Writing includes many forms that foster discovery, reflection, idea development, and expression.
▸ Writing is most effective when it is created in a process that includes actionable feedback.

Writing attitudes can impact learning performance:

▸ Writing ability and feelings of self-efficacy are mutually reinforcing.
▸ Writing perceptions increase or inhibit our voluntary exposure to learning opportunities.

Ultimately, Savannah State University's cross-campus utilization of writing as a tool for education allows us to matriculate graduates of higher learning that are equipped to contribute creative and critical thought through written communication to the global community and marketplace.

It is evident that the student authors in this *International Marketing and Management Research* book series (Volume 3) have benefitted from educational environments and dedicated teachers that encourage and promote their development as thinkers, researchers, and writers. It is from this strong foundation that they have been equipped to significantly add to the confluence of advertising, as an evolution of the world of marketing communications into social movements.

DOI: 10.1057/9781137492265.0016

Index

DOI: 10.1057/9781137492265.0017

DOI: 10.1057/9781137492265.0017

DOI: 10.1057/9781137492265.0017

GPSR Compliance
The European Union's (EU) General Product Safety Regulation (GPSR) is a set
of rules that requires consumer products to be safe and our obligations to
ensure this.

If you have any concerns about our products, you can contact us on

ProductSafety@springernature.com

In case Publisher is established outside the EU, the EU authorized
representative is:

Springer Nature Customer Service Center GmbH
Europaplatz 3
69115 Heidelberg, Germany